Selling your Pharmacy for all it's worth

Selling your Pharmacy

for all it's worth

The guide to selling your
community pharmacy business

Anne Hutchings

Matador
9 Priory Business Park
Kibworth Beauchamp
Leicestershire LE8 0RX, UK
Tel: (+44) 116 279 2299
Fax: (+44) 116 279 2277
Email: books@troubador.co.uk
Web: www.troubador.co.uk/matador

ISBN 978 1784622 411

British Library Cataloguing in Publication Data.
A catalogue record for this book is available from the British Library.

Typeset in Garamond by Troubador Publishing Ltd
Printed and bound in the UK by TJ International, Padstow, Cornwall

Matador is an imprint of Troubador Publishing Ltd

The views and opinions of the author are her own. The author will not be held liable for anyone acting on information or advice given in the book since individual circumstances can vary. If you are undertaking the sale of a pharmacy and unsure of the actions you need to undertake, you should seek professional advice. Readers should also note that the facts relating to tax and legislation may no longer be current and market circumstances may have changed.

Hutchings Consultants Ltd, Maple House,
53-55 Woodside Road,
Amersham, Bucks HP6 6AA
Tel: 01494 722224 Fax: 01494 434764
Email: anne@hutchingsconsultants.com

Contents

About the Author

Anne Hutchings is a tax consultant by profession. Over the past two decades she has built up a successful accountancy and tax practice specialising in the retail pharmacy market.

This specialisation in the pharmacy sector led clients to ask her for assistance with both buying and selling pharmacies. Anne identified a gap in the market and rather than just dabble in this area when clients asked for help she set up a separate pharmacy brokerage business dealing with pharmacy sales and valuations.

The key to the success of this business has been the in-house tax and accountancy knowledge she can offer, which ensures that clients maximise their sale proceeds. No other pharmacy agent can offer this breadth of expertise, she believes.

Over the past 12 years Hutchings Consultants Ltd has grown to be the largest independent pharmacy sales agents in the UK.

Anne Hutchings and Hutchings Consultants Ltd are based in Amersham, Buckinghamshire (www.hutchingsconsultants.com).

About the Author

Introduction

If you own a pharmacy you will, at some point, start to think about selling it. It's a natural progression but it is also a huge step – one of the biggest and most important you are ever likely to make. Most pharmacists only sell a business once so it is something you need to get right first time: you want to get the best price and negotiate terms that suit you.

Selling a pharmacy can be a minefield for the uninitiated, yet many pharmacy owners approach the task with a frightening lack of focus and little forethought or planning. As a pharmacy agent I have seen many sales fail to complete because pharmacists try to handle the process themselves without proper help and support and come unstuck.

At present demand for pharmacy businesses is high. It is a sellers' market and this can make pharmacy owners complacent - they think that it will be easy to sell their business. It may look like an easy option when a private buyer makes you an offer, particularly if it's someone you know such as your locum or another local proprietor. There's an element of trust, you know the person and they are a fellow pharmacist ... what could go wrong! Sadly a sale is rarely straightforward. Lots of things can and do go wrong, from selling the business for less than it's worth to structuring the sale in a way which ends up costing you many thousands of unnecessary pounds in tax.

It was the observation that private sales frequently collapse after many stressful months for all involved that inspired me to write this book. I hope it provides an informative, educational and cautionary read for those contemplating selling a pharmacy. If it serves to prevent some pharmacy owners from making poor decisions and loosing substantial amounts of money when selling their business I will have achieved my goal.

Where do you start? This book guides you through the steps of the sales process and outlines some of the important decisions you need to make on the way. If you follow the advice and tips given it should save you many thousands of pounds. The purpose of the book is to act as an eye opener to the issues involved in the sale and encourage you to take the right actions to maximise your sale proceeds.

Anne Hutchings, January 2015

CHAPTER 1

Is it time to sell?

Is it time to sell your pharmacy? Is selling up the right thing to do? Ultimately only you can answer these questions, but having talked to hundreds of pharmacy owners over the years I know what difficult decisions these can be. Your primary reason for selling may be one of the following:

Feeling tired and worn out

'Burn out' can hit you at any stage of your career. It may come as a surprise but I have dealt with many young pharmacists who have sold up because they feel worn out, and want to get out of pharmacy to do something else. If you are no longer enjoying everyday life as a pharmacy owner then serious consideration should be given to selling – after all you only live once! Quality of life is important and as a large part of our time is spent in the work environment it can be miserable if you no longer enjoy it.

Increasing legislative burden

Many pharmacy owners become disillusioned because of constant regulatory changes and the massive amount of legislation their business has to comply with. "I no longer have time to be a pharmacist: most of my time is taken up with form filling and bureaucracy" is a typical complaint.

Retirement

There are no age restrictions to stop a pharmacist practising so deciding when to retire can be a difficult decision, particularly if you are healthy and still enjoy running your business. I have sold pharmacies for people in their eighties. As an interim step before full retirement some pharmacists sell their business but continue to work as a locum. This frees up some time for relaxation, removes the stress of having to run the business and enables them to do what they became a pharmacist for: help their patients.

Poor health
It is unfortunate when a pharmacy owner has to sell up because of poor health, whether it is personal or illness in the family. The thought process then turns to how to best structure and handle the sale with minimum stress for all concerned.

Change of lifestyle
Pharmacists sometimes sell up so that they can start a new business or career. Selling the pharmacy can be a way to fund this change of direction.

Cashing in the goodwill
Nobody knows what the future holds for community pharmacy. In this uncertain world sometimes pharmacy owners just think the time is right to cash in the goodwill and invest the proceeds elsewhere.

When is the best time to sell?

If you have decided to sell, the best time to do so is when your pharmacy is desirable and likely to attract a number of good offers. Over the past few years, with 100-hour contracts and the drift of doctors into health centres, there has been a lot of uncertainty in the market. However, now the threat of new 100-hour contracts has been removed, there is renewed confidence and buyers are again out in force.

The ideal time to sell is when there are no direct threats to your business that could affect its goodwill value. If there is a potential problem, you should still be able to sell but be prepared to accept a lower price or deferred payments – or both – to reflect the situation.

Market conditions
Factors such as interest rates, the availability of credit, the tax regime, industry confidence and government legislation are outside your control.

However, two key factors for pharmacy buyers are interest rates and availability of credit. Banks are generally keen to lend to pharmacy buyers and interest rates have been at historically low levels. This makes acquiring a pharmacy attractive to buyers, and is helpful if you are looking to sell.

The tax rates on a business sale are also favourable at the moment, making it a good time to sell from a tax perspective. For most pharmacy sellers the situation is fairly straightforward: providing you qualify for Entrepreneur's Relief – and most pharmacy owners do – you will only pay 10 per cent capital gains tax on the sale of your business. For example, a pharmacy sold with a capital gain of £1 million would have a tax bill of £100,000 if taxed at the current rate of 10 per cent.

Industry trends
The environment in which pharmacies operate, both as high street retailers and NHS contractors, is constantly evolving. The counter trade in most pharmacies has diminished substantially in recent years with most businesses now seeing no more than 10 per cent of their turnover coming from the front shop. The emphasis is on delivering health services to increase income. This can be positive for buyers if their target pharmacy is not providing such services as it gives them scope to develop the business.

Consolidation of GP practices has had a significant effect on the dispensing business of many pharmacies. The opening of a health centre with a pharmacy on-site can have a devastating effect on nearby community pharmacies.

In England the opening of 100-hour contract pharmacies has had a considerable impact on existing pharmacy businesses. Between 2005 and 2012 there were 2,484 applications for 100-hour contracts, of which around 88 per cent were granted. Many pharmacy owners breathed a sigh of relief when it was announced that no new 100-hour contracts would be considered.

While the debate around 100-hour pharmacies has hogged the headlines there has been little publicity about mail order and internet pharmacies which also pose a threat to traditional 'bricks and mortar' businesses. Distance selling pharmacies can supply NHS prescriptions to anyone as long the person does not visit the pharmacy premises. This has opened the door for these pharmacies to target nursing and residential homes, as well as providing collection and delivery services in local communities.

The squeeze on government spending has inevitably had an effect on income from NHS pharmacy services. Despite an ageing population and a year-on-year increase in prescription items pharmacy turnover has remained fairly static in recent years. As evidenced by the October 2014 remuneration settlement, pharmacists seem to be expected to work harder for no increase in remuneration!

Most pharmacies now offer prescription collection services from their local surgeries and in many cases are also providing a delivery service to anyone that wants it. This demonstrates the competition in the market place for NHS prescription business. It has an impact on the profits of those pharmacies as the cost of providing vehicles and drivers to deliver these services has to be met.

Despite all these issues pharmacy goodwill values are holding up. This is largely because a well run pharmacy is still a good profitable business and the demand by far exceeds the supply, creating a seller's market. What does the future hold for goodwill value? Without knowing what plans the government has for the NHS it is difficult to predict, but in the absence of any new legislation to tighten margins, there is no reason for prices to fall. So are prices likely to increase any further in the near future? Again, this is difficult to predict, but I see no reason why they should unless there is a marked boost in NHS funding which seems unlikely.

Other factors
It can be a good time to sell when you are near to retirement and the business is at a point where it needs money spent on it, such as a refit or a new computer system. I am often asked: 'Should I spend money on a refit before I sell?' I would usually advise that it is not worth it – better to let the new owner do it. Buyers will not normally pay extra for fixtures and fittings, so if you have just spent £50,000 on a refit you are not going to see £50,000 added to the sale price.

How much of your money is tied up in the pharmacy? Often the pharmacy and your home will be your main assets. Having a large part of your wealth tied up in a business when you are nearing retirement can be risky if the goodwill values suddenly drop or tax rates increase. It can make sense to sell at a time when there are plenty of buyers and you can obtain a fair return for your hard work.

Is now a good time to sell?

If you are thinking of selling I believe now is a good time for various reasons:

- The lack of pharmacies for sale compared with a huge number of buyers is positive for anyone thinking of selling. If you have a desirable pharmacy, expect several offers.
- There are low tax rates on the sale proceeds. Providing you qualify for Entrepreneur's Relief, a 10 per cent charge on your capital gain is very attractive. You have to wonder if this relief will be a future target for a government short of funds!
- If your business is doing well and there are no negative issues affecting it, then it's a good time to sell. Unfortunately

pharmacy owners sometimes decide to sell when a situation develops that will adversely affect the business, such as the relocation of a nearby GP surgery. Where there is uncertainty surrounding a sale it not only puts buyers off, but can have a substantial impact on the value of the business.

When considering what you are going to do you should think through the financial aspects. If you are thinking of retiring, will you have enough money to fund your future lifestyle? If there is a shortfall, how can you overcome this? Are you clear about how you are going to invest the proceeds from the sale? When I talk to potential pharmacy sellers they sometimes tell me that while they want to sell they don't know what to do with the proceeds. If you are unsure about your investment options speak to a good independent financial adviser and your accountant.

Whatever your reason for selling, you need to be absolutely sure that it is right decision for you. Whether or not to sell your business will be one of the biggest decisions you ever make, and once your pharmacy has been sold there is no going back! You should have clear reasons for selling and clear objectives for what you want to achieve in the future. Think carefully about what you are going to do when you have sold up. I have had pharmacy sales fall through when the owner has suddenly panicked at the prospect of having nothing to do once the business has gone!

The pharmacy community is a small one, and word gets around quickly. Buyers will remember if you put your pharmacy on the market and later changed your mind and withdrew it. Your business will be tarnished and its future value may be affected. The way that buyers see it is that the business was for sale, but didn't sell, so there must be something wrong with it. When it appears on the market again, perhaps a year or so later, they will remember and steer clear of it.

Key points for a successful sale

1. Be clear about the reasons why you are selling.

2. Understand your financial position and what you are going to do with the proceeds from the sale.

3. Be 100 per cent committed to selling.

CHAPTER 2

How much is my pharmacy worth?

When prospective sellers call me often the first thing they ask is: 'What will I get to the pound these days?' In years gone by 'pence in the pound' was commonly used as a rough guide to the value of a business, although even then it had flaws. Today things have changed. You can no longer just look at a 'pence in the pound' figure: far more emphasis is put on pharmacy profits. There are also other factors that affect a pharmacy's value. But first, an illustration to show why 'pence in the pound' is not an accurate measure for valuing a pharmacy.

Take the accounts of two pharmacies, both with a £1 million turnover:

	Pharmacy A	*Pharmacy B*
Sales (turnover)	*£1,000,000*	*£1,000,000*
Gross profit	*£300,000*	*£300,000*
Trading expenses	*£150,000*	*£250,000*
Net profit	**£150,000**	**£50,000**

Is pharmacy B, with a net profit of only £50,000, really going to be worth as much as pharmacy A with net profits of £150,000?

If you are selling a pharmacy, your business will be valued by both the buyer and their lender based on its profitability. However, some desirable pharmacies in certain locations will command a premium price, and this will be discussed in more detail later.

When someone asks me what their pharmacy is worth, the first thing I do is to ask to see their latest set of accounts and up-to-date trading figures. This is how a lender – usually a bank – will value the business and the buyer will make an offer based on this information.

I also ask the pharmacy owner some key questions to get an overall feel for the business so that I can establish how desirable it will be when it goes on the market.

A typical set of pharmacy accounts

Mr Patel, who is a sole trader in Leicester, wants to sell the pharmacy that he has owned and managed for the last 10 years. The key figures from his latest accounts are as follows:

Sales – NHS	*£800,000*
Sales – Counter	*£80,000*
Total sales	*£880,000*
Cost of sales	*£624,800*
Gross profit	*£255,200*
Trading expenses	*£129,000*
EBITDA*	***£126,200***

*Earnings Before Interest, Tax, Depreciation, and Amortization

When calculating EBITDA remember to include a full market salary for yourself if you are working in the pharmacy. When calculating a market value for the business the banks will typically take a multiple of the EBITDA ranging from around five to seven times.

If it was 5 x £126,200 the value would be £631,000.
If it was 7 x £126,200 the value would be £883,400.

At this point the pharmacy is expected to be worth somewhere between £631,000 and £883,000, with the pharmacy owner obviously hoping for a figure close to £883,000 or even more!

What determines value?

Location, location, location...
Unsurprisingly, a pharmacy located in a health centre or next door to a GP surgery would generally expect to command a higher price.

Pharmacies in some parts of the UK are more sought after than others. Businesses in places that are regarded as a bit out of the way, such as Cornwall, may struggle to sell simply because there is not the demand. On the other hand, businesses in London and the Home Counties are highly sought after.

Threats to the viability
In England those areas where a lot of 100-hour contracts have been granted have become less desirable. More specifically, a 100-hour contract pharmacy that has opened up near enough to your pharmacy to affect its business can have a significant impact on its value, and could even make it difficult to sell. Similarly, GP relocation in an area can adversely affect the value of a pharmacy and limit the interest of potential buyers.

Staff costs
One of the biggest factors affecting valuations that I am seeing at the moment is where businesses have staff costs that are higher than the norm for pharmacies of a similar size. Staff wages impact on net profit, and if a pharmacy is overstaffed it will act to reduce the sale value of the business. Nine times out of ten business owners are aware that their pharmacy is overstaffed but they don't want to do anything about it – they are about to sell and don't want to rock the boat. When I raise this, the typical response is: 'The new owner can sort it out.'

That may be the case, but overstaffing will reduce the value of your business and limit the interest from potential buyers. A new owner does not want to begin their tenure by making people redundant. It is costly, time consuming and will affect the relationship between staff and the new management.

If you are thinking of selling in the next few years, have a good look at your staff costs. I was working with a health centre pharmacy recently where I reviewed the business and advised them on issues which affected its value, one of which was staff costs. A target date was set to get everything in order, including a reduction in staff hours, and I estimate this put an extra £200,000 on the value of that pharmacy.

Property leases

High rents, unreasonable terms in the lease, or leases which are not renewable, are all issues that will affect the value of a pharmacy. Buyers need security of tenure and will be looking for a lease with at least 10 years left and that is renewable at the end of the term. Sometimes lenders will be looking for leases of more than 10 years.

If you have a lease make sure it is in order before the pharmacy goes on the market. If you have a lease which is not renewable you may find that you cannot find a buyer for the business, particularly if the lease has less than 10 years left.

The size of premises

Are your premises big enough for the business? Sometimes I see pharmacies with sizeable turnovers operating from small premises – there may not even be enough space for a proper consultation room. If there isn't the space to offer new services, take on more staff and increase the turnover it can limit the potential of the business.

A new owner will want a business with a future, so size limitations can affect the value of your pharmacy. If this applies to you, what can you do about it? If there is room to expand it may be worth looking into. Alternatively, if there are other suitable premises nearby it may be worth relocating. If your pharmacy has limited floor space it may just be worth exploring your options.

Nature of the business
The value of your pharmacy may be affected if a substantial part of your dispensing business comes from supplying nursing or residential homes. As a general guide, if more than 10 per cent of your NHS items come from care homes then this needs to be taken into account in any valuation.

Dealing with homes can be 'easy come, easy go'. When I ask owners who have recently bought a pharmacy dealing with care homes how things are going, I often hear that they lost the homes not long after they took over the business. Dealing with care homes is also labour intensive. If you are supplying homes have a look at what you are earning from them and calculate your costs to see what profit, if any, you are making.

The supply of medicines in monitored dosage systems (MDS) can also be labour intensive, so I would also look at whether this type of supply accounts for more than 10-12 per cent of turnover.

I still occasionally encounter pharmacies, usually in city centres, with a high OTC turnover. These days the counter trade in most pharmacies accounts for no more than about 10 per cent of turnover. A pharmacy that has a particularly high counter trade will see this reflected in its valuation, since buyers are not keen on paying for business that might not be sustainable. Lenders also tend to look closely at this part of the business, and will tighten their lending criteria for pharmacies where the counter trade makes up more than 25 per cent of turnover. This, in turn, has a negative effect on offers you may receive from buyers.

Potential for growth
If you are buying a pharmacy you want one with potential for development. Consequently pharmacies with growth potential are more popular with buyers and likely to sell at a premium since

they will attract more competitive offers. If you are going to sell your pharmacy it is a good idea to stand back and take a long hard look at it from a buyer's perspective. If you were starting out again, what would you do to enhance and grow the business? Make a list of all the 'selling points' you can identify to present to your buyers.

Wholesale and internet business
Many pharmacies now receive some income from wholesaling or internet sales in their turnover. Often it is difficult to separate the income from the wholesale and internet parts of the business from that of the traditional pharmacy, and this can cause problems with a valuation.

My experience of selling pharmacies has shown that buyers don't want to pay for wholesaling activity, so this needs to be taken out of the equation. But if a buyer can't easily see what the make-up of the business is, they will not bother with it and move on.

I can't stress enough the importance of asking your accountant to prepare a simple but separate profit and loss account for any wholesaling or internet business you carry out. Internet pharmacy sales can incur high levels of expenses. Lumping this in with your main pharmacy business income and expenses may be fine for HMRC, but it will not help in presenting the business in the most attractive way to a buyer!

Financial information
You cannot sell your business without up-to-date financial information. Long gone are the days when you could produce accounts that were a couple of years out of date. Both buyers and their lenders expect to see the latest accounts. If you are selling a group they will be looking for management accounts for the current year as well as individual profit and loss accounts for each branch. If this financial information is not available you may struggle to sell the business or perhaps only attract one or two poor offers – in other words you are leaving money on the table.

Trading hours

If a pharmacy is open for more than about 55 hours a week it will start to have a negative impact on any valuation. The more hours a pharmacy is open the higher the staff costs will be, which in turn will reflect in the bottom line profit and hence the pharmacy's value. Pharmacies in London, where longer hours are expected and accepted, are an exception to this rule.

100-hour pharmacies

You may be wondering what the situation is with 100-hour pharmacies. Are they viable? Can you sell them, and what are they worth?

There has been much debate on the point at which 100-hour pharmacies become viable and start to turn in a profit. As a general guide once turnover reaches around £1 million the business will move into profit, although I have sold 100-hour pharmacies with a lower turnover that were profitable. Providing they are profitable 100-hour pharmacies can be sold, and they have become more desirable since a stop has been put on any new 100-hour contracts. If you have a 100-hour pharmacy in a health centre turning over a couple of million pounds a year it should be quite easy to sell, and you should attract a number of offers.

However, a 100-hour pharmacy is worth considerably less than one with a standard hours contract. All the points above regarding pharmacy valuations will still apply but as a rough guide a 100-hour pharmacy is likely to achieve a market value of 50-80 per cent of a business that has a standard hours contract.

What is the business worth?

Having looked at things that will affect the value of a pharmacy, let's go back to Mr Patel in Leicester. The true net profit of his pharmacy (EBITDA) was £126,200. When valuing a business, a lender will typically take a multiple of this ranging from around five to seven times.

If it was 5 x £126,200 the value would be £631,000
If it was 7 x £126,200 the value would be £883,400

So let's look at the factors which will help to determine the value of Mr Patel's pharmacy. The pharmacy is in a good secondary location with other shops and good parking serving the local community. It has no direct competition, the nearest pharmacy being over a mile away. Leicester is a popular location for pharmacy buyers, so this is all positive.

Mr Patel is not aware of anything happening in the area which could affect his business. The nearest GP surgery, from which most of the dispensing business derives, is about 300 metres away and there is no likelihood of it moving.

The accounts show that staff costs were £45,000 (excluding a pharmacist salary) which is reasonable for the size of the business. There are 12 years left on a 15 year lease under the Landlord and Tenant Act, which means it should be renewable at the end of the term. The business rent and rates of £20,000 per annum are reasonable.

The premises are a double fronted shop with a large floor area, a good size dispensary, and a consultation room and stock room at the rear. There is plenty of room for a new owner to take in more prescriptions and develop services.

Mr Patel runs a typical pharmacy. It is open 45 hours a week, and turnover is split about 90 per cent NHS and 10 per cent OTC. Mr Patel doesn't deal with any nursing or residential care homes, and MDS is negligible. He has not embraced any opportunities to deliver local Enhanced or Advanced Services so there is potential to develop these.

There are a number of care homes in the area which a new owner could approach. The pharmacy's script collection service is limited to just the nearby surgery so this, along with a delivery service, could be developed.

Mr Patel hasn't embraced internet pharmacy either, and has no wholesaling activities, so his accounts, which are available and up to date, are transparent.

Overall everything is positive for Mr Patel, so based on my knowledge of the market I would recommend marketing the business for offers of over £880,000 for the goodwill. This is pitched at a level which should create competitive interest and I would expect to achieve several good offers from which I can negotiate the best price.

Premium prices

No one can tell exactly how much a pharmacy will sell for on the open market. What I can tell you is that you will kill any interest in a business if you put it on the market at a price that is too high. I have had people come to me who have had their pharmacy up for sale with another agent for over a year and haven't been able to sell it. When I have looked at the valuation I frequently find the business has been marketed at a price that is far too high.

Recently I have seen a substantial premium being paid for desirable pharmacies. It is key to put the business on the market at a guide price that will attract buyers and then let them decide on the value through competitive bidding and negotiation. Some pharmacies sell for far in excess of bank valuations so unless you put your pharmacy on the open market you will never know what its true value is. I recently advised on the sale of a pharmacy in South London. The vendor received ten offers and sold for 62 per cent more than the guide price. Going back to Mr Patel's pharmacy, I would expect it to fetch well in excess of the guide price if it was properly marketed.

Key points for a successful sale

1. Have a professional valuation done by a pharmacy expert. Don't try and guess what your pharmacy may be worth. It is probably one of the biggest assets you will ever sell in your life, so don't sell yourself short.

2. Make sure your financial information is up to date and available. Lack of information makes it difficult to carry out an accurate valuation.

CHAPTER 3

Can I improve my valuation?

This chapter falls into two parts. The first part is for those who are thinking of selling now, while the second is for those who are looking to sell in the next two to five years. But whether you are selling now or later, to achieve the best price for your business you must make sure it is prepared for sale.

If you are planning to sell now the best thing you can do is to make sure that your financial accounts are up-to-date. If buyers have to wait for information they will lose interest and any offers you receive will be low, based on the lack of information. Poor information will reduce the value of your pharmacy. You would also be advised to review the areas of the business listed below:

Gross profit
One of the first things a buyer will look at is gross profit. You should know what your gross profit percentage is, but have you any idea of whether this is high or low compared with other pharmacies? If the pharmacy is underperforming by industry standards it will affect the price you obtain when you sell.

Stock
Are you carrying too much stock? Buyers will sometimes put a cap on how much stock they are prepared to take. An experienced buyer will know what the stock levels should be for your type of pharmacy. Do you?

Contracts and leases
Review any documentation to ensure there are no problem areas

when you come to sell. For example, make sure all your staff have contracts of employment which meet legal requirements, and that the minimum wage legislation is being met. Any equipment leases should be checked to make sure they can be transferred to a new owner if required, and that there are no potential issues which could cause a dispute with the buyer.

If the pharmacy premises are leasehold make sure that the lease meets the criteria buyers will expect (this is covered in more detail in Chapter 8).

Costs

Go through your pharmacy expenses carefully and see if there are areas where you can reduce your expenditure.

Staff wages: As a guideline staff wages (excluding a pharmacist salary) should not be more than about 6 per cent of your turnover. A pharmacist salary will account for a further 6 per cent. This is a rough guide and won't apply to all pharmacies, such as those with a low turnover, or that are open for long hours. If you are overstaffed your options are:

- To leave things unchanged. This will be reflected in your goodwill value. For example, if you could realistically reduce your staff costs by £20,000 you could add at least £100,000 to the value of your pharmacy.
- Make redundancies. This is never an easy option and you would be advised to seek legal advice to ensure the correct procedures are followed.
- If a staff member leaves or retires consider whether it is viable to operate without replacing them.

Owner's expenses: The higher your expenses, the lower your profit will be. This reduces your tax bill, which works well while you own the business. However, when you come to sell a lower profit means a lower price from the buyer. If you have expenses in your accounts which may not necessarily continue with a new owner, such as salaries for family members or personal motor expenses, either take them out of your accounts or list them clearly for any prospective buyer.

Potential

Buyers are looking for a business that has potential. Many of the pharmacies that I sell have been under the same ownership for years, with the pharmacist now coming up to retirement. These businesses usually have the potential to improve their turnover and profit. Take the time to make a list of all the things a new owner could do to develop the business.

Thinking ahead

If your business is growing and you are expecting turnover to increase in the next year it is worth preparing a projection of turnover and profits for the next 12 months. Ask your accountant to do this for you if you don't have the time or expertise to do it yourself.

Minimise tax

If you trade through a limited company there are often ways in which you can reduce the tax on the sale of your pharmacy. You should discuss this with a tax expert who specialises in pharmacy.

Finally, selling a business can be distracting, so don't take your eye off the ball! Make sure you continue to focus on running the business and surround yourself with experts who can take the pressure off you with regard to the sale. A sale can take months to complete and during that time you need to at least maintain if not improve the business performance. A buyer will quickly pick up on falling revenue, giving them an excuse to re-negotiate on the price.

Selling in two to five years

If you are thinking about selling in the next few years it is never too soon to start planning. In addition to the points already covered you should also look at your business in more detail:

Stage 1: What is the business worth now?

Stage 2: What do you need to do to minimise the tax on the sale? (See Chapter 4)

Stage 3: What could the business be worth in two, three or five years if you grow the business by X per cent per annum (decide your time scale and percentage growth target)

Stage 4: What do you need to do to get from stage 1 to stage 3?

A good starting point is to carry out a SWOT analysis. This is an in-depth examination of the pharmacy's strengths and weaknesses, and the opportunities and threats it faces. Preparing a summary of these will help you identify the areas you need to work on to make your business more attractive to buyers. Parts of the business that you might want to review as a result of this could include:

Business structure
Consider the different elements of what you are selling, such as goodwill, company shares, and freehold property. If you own a company are there assets in it other than the pharmacy? I often advise clients to 'clean the company up' prior to a sale since buyers will not want to purchase the other investments you may have accumulated under the company umbrella. You can take investments and properties out of your company prior to sale, but there are tax considerations and you could end up with a large tax bill without proper tax advice. If you have accumulated cash in your company there are opportunities for tax planning, so don't just take the cash out – take advice.

Business performance and costs
There are four key areas to look at if you want to improve profits. These are business strategy, marketing, financial controls and business management.

Business strategy The first step is to take some time out from the pharmacy and make an objective assessment of the business. Draw up a strategic plan for the period of time up until you intend to sell the business. This will typically include how the business might look at the time when you come to sell it. You should incorporate:

- The services and products provided to your customers.
- Your customer base and geographical area.
- The size of your business, including turnover, gross margin, profitability, number of retail outlets, and staffing requirements.

Part of the process should include a financial plan to show business growth and profitability. For pharmacy businesses the key figures to include are:

- Turnover, broken down into NHS and OTC
- Gross profit
- Business expenses
- Net profit.

Include an estimate of the goodwill value now and at the time when you are ready to sell.

How does this plan help increase profits? It makes you recognise where you are now, and where you want to be in the future when you come to sell the business. It should help you to identify what you need to do to get there.

Marketing Have a look at your accounts from the past few years. Has your turnover been increasing, decreasing or staying much the same? Buyers are looking for a solid business which they can develop further. If you have a couple of years or so before you sell work on a marketing plan to increase your turnover. What are you doing to attract more customers and to retain the existing ones? As part of your strategic plan you will have reviewed your customer base and your customers' needs. Did you also look at where your prescriptions come from, the location of GP surgeries and your relationship with local doctors? Is there anything in the pipeline that could affect future script numbers? Other points to consider are:

- Location. Taking into account the restrictions imposed by the Control of Entry Regulations, is your business in the best location? Bearing in mind competitors, doctors and customers, are there any options open to you for improving your location? If you do consider moving you need to budget for all the costs involved and balance these against your estimate of any resulting increase in trade and value on selling the business.

- Existing products and services. Make a list of the main product categories you sell, and within them the product lines you keep in stock. Have a look at the turnover of these monthly, quarterly and annually. What is the gross profit margin? Does your stock accurately reflect the needs of your customers? Which are your fast moving lines and which are the most profitable? Could stocking other brands increase the gross profit? Look at your merchandising and product displays. Are the products placed to best advantage to obtain maximum sales?

- NHS dispensing. For most pharmacies the prescription side of the business accounts for the largest part of turnover by value. Are the prescriptions you dispense mainly for NHS patients? Do you dispense any private scripts? Do you provide services for drug addicts or nursing homes? Some pharmacists do not wish to provide services for addicts, but if you do it can help to increase your gross margin.

- Care home services may or may not be profitable. Before taking on a nursing or residential home carefully work out what it will cost you to service it. Don't forget to include staff time and delivery costs in terms of drivers and vehicle costs. If you already deal with care homes isolate the turnover applicable to them, calculate the gross margin and then deduct the costs applicable and see how profitable this work is. Pharmacy owners are often surprised to discover that the nursing home services they provide are actually loss making.

What other services do you provide? What could you provide? Perhaps you have surplus space in your premises that could be rented out to other healthcare service providers.

Train your staff to ask customers the right questions. By making sure that their needs are met customers will feel that they have received an excellent service and this will help to build loyalty. At the same time, by fully understanding your customers' requirements, additional sales can be made.

An electronic point of sale system could be a key element in increasing your profits. Many community pharmacists dismiss EPoS because of the cost and time needed to effectively implement such a system. However, the benefits and savings that can be achieved should far outweigh these two factors. The key benefits are:

- Improved cash flow.
- Improved gross margin.
- Automatic re-ordering of stock.
- Low profit areas highlighted: what is and isn't selling.
- Pre-set reports providing analysis of profit margins and highlighting shrinkage.
- Price monitoring and quick implementation of price changes.
- Identification of over and under stocking of products and lost sales.

Customer loyalty schemes are a way of encouraging customers to return regularly to your pharmacy. There are a number of different ways in which these can work. One example is to have a points system, where points are earned every time the customer purchases items in the shop. These points can be redeemed at certain times of the year by way of discount against other items purchased.

Advertise your business by producing leaflets to hand out to customers in the pharmacy, doing a leaflet drop to local residents, and placing adverts in local papers. The leaflets can be informative or used to advertise specific products or services. Do you advertise your business on the internet?

Give the business a facelift. When did the pharmacy last have a refit? Many pharmacies have not been refitted for years and look tired and shabby. Most successful pharmacy owners carry out refits regularly, often around every seven years. There is no question this increases trade and, therefore, profitability. However, if you are planning to sell within the next three or four years it is unlikely that it will be a cost effective option for you.

If this is the case, at least have an objective look at your premises. Start from the outside. Is it the sort of place you would want to shop in? Are the windows clean and is the paintwork smart? How does it look inside? Is it old and shabby, or clean and tidy? What can you do to improve the image? When was the last time the shop was decorated? Are the floor coverings worn? As a healthcare provider and with increasing competition all these points are important. You want customers to enjoy the experience of visiting your premises so that they return again.

Financial controls

The starting point is to review your accounting system. Whether you do the bookkeeping yourself or employ an outside bookkeeper, your system must allow you to extract certain key data. A basic bookkeeping system will enable you to produce monthly VAT returns and reclaim VAT, which is good for cash flow.

One way of increasing your profit is to have a good financial management system in place. This will consist of a computerised bookkeeping system with data input by someone appropriately skilled. There is no point in having a system that contains incorrect information, or a software package that you do not understand and from which you cannot extract the relevant figures.

When I carry out pharmacy valuations I ask for copies of the VAT returns, and find that in about a quarter of cases they have been incorrectly completed! What do you think buyers will make of this? At the very least it will cast doubt on the accuracy of any other financial information that is provided to them. One way of dealing with this issue is to have a bookkeeper or accountant who sets up the system, inputs all the information and provides you with the key figures and reports each month. This means you can utilise your time, both working in and on the business, in a more effective way.

Once you have the basic financial information you need, you can use this to help improve business performance by:

- Accurately measuring how you are doing. Ask your accountant to benchmark your business against other pharmacies.
- Monitoring and controlling your costs.
- Forecasting ahead and preparing budgets for forthcoming expenditure.
- Monitoring progress. If you have set a target to increase your gross margin by X per cent, you can monitor the effectiveness of your efforts through your monthly financial data.
- Using the data for 'what if?' scenarios. For example, by how much will your gross and net profit increase if you:

  - increase your OTC sales by 10 per cent next year?
  - increase your NHS items by 7 per cent?
  - reduce your staff costs by 5 per cent?
  - take on two new nursing homes?
  - let the spare room at the back of the pharmacy to a chiropodist?

If you are adept at using spreadsheets you can set up a format to do the calculations for you – if not ask your accountant to do it.

Business management

Effective management of the business will improve your profit. Why? Because businesses with proper systems in place operate more efficiently and provide a better quality of customer service. How successful a community pharmacy is will depend on how good the management is in supplying its customers' needs on a timely basis in a pleasant environment, with the aid of helpful and knowledgeable staff.

Part of the management process involves setting standards and putting procedures in place for everyone in the business to follow. Pharmacists will be familiar with the General Pharmaceutical Council's requirement for standard operating procedures (SOPs) and will appreciate that they are a good way of implementing tighter management controls.

The overall benefit of SOPs is that they allow you to introduce systems and procedures into your pharmacy that help it run more efficiently and enable your staff to carry out their work to a consistent standard. It may be an appropriate time to review your SOPs. Discuss them with your staff and see how they can be improved.

Unfortunately there is no simple way to massively increase profits. It takes a systematic approach involving good business management, financial monitoring, successful marketing and a strategy for your business. If you find the prospect of tackling all these items together too daunting, break it down into small chunks.

Start by drawing up a plan of action that you can use to review and improve your business. It is important to include review points, actions you will take and the dates by which you plan to complete tasks. The important point about having a written action plan with deadlines is that it will help you focus on the tasks and work to a specific timescale.

Key points for a successful sale

1. Start preparing for sale as early as possible.

2. Conduct a thorough review of the business, looking for ways in which you can make it more valuable and attractive to buyers. It should be money well spent to engage a pharmacy specialist to do this for you.

3. Create a plan of action for maximising the pharmacy value and act on it.

CHAPTER 4

Tax matters

It's not just the price you receive for selling your business that is important, but how much you are left with after tax. If you are selling up and want to achieve the maximum return you need good tax advice. Pharmacy owners who are thinking of selling should ask not only how much they can get for their pharmacy, but how much tax they will have to pay. Nine out of ten pharmacists that I speak to have not considered their tax position, yet the correct structuring of a sale can sometimes save not just thousands but hundreds of thousands of pounds in tax.

This chapter looks at tax considerations for both sole traders/partnerships and for companies. It is a general guide and is not a substitute for taking professional advice from a tax expert.

Sole traders and partnerships

If you are a sole trader or partnership your tax position should be relatively straightforward. Your main question is how much tax you are going end up paying on the sale of your pharmacy? The answer is that you will pay capital gains tax on the sale proceeds of the business after deducting the acquisition cost and incidental expenses relating to its sale and purchase.

Capital gains can be taxed at rates of up to 28 per cent. The good news is that most business owners can benefit from Entrepreneurs' Relief (ER) on the first £10 million of gains made on disposal of their business. This allows gains of up to £10 million to be taxed at an effective rate of 10 per cent. Gains in excess of this will be taxed at the standard capital gains rates.

As a pharmacy owner selling a pharmacy business you should qualify for ER providing you have owned the business for at least one year. If you own more than one business ER can be claimed on more than one occasion, however a lifetime limit of £10 million will apply. The following example illustrates how ER works in practice:

Jack has two pharmacies eligible for ER. The first pharmacy is sold in May 2014 with a capital gain of £1.5 million, and the second pharmacy is sold the following year with a capital gain of £1 million.

First pharmacy sale	*Capital gain £1,500,000*	
Capital gains tax payable at 10 per cent		**£150,000**
Second pharmacy sale	*Capital gain £1,000,000*	
Maximum ER allowable		*£10 million*
Less previously claimed		*£1.5 million*
Balance of ER available		*£8.5 million*

Therefore the second pharmacy qualifies in full for ER.

Capital gains tax payable at 10 per cent	**£100,000**
Total tax payable on gains of £2.5 million	**£250,000**

If you own the premises from which the business trades and sell this with the pharmacy the property may also qualify for ER. If so, it will also form part of your lifetime allowance of £10 million. The rules regarding property are complicated and where, for example, a property has been let to a partnership by one or more of the business partners ER relief may be restricted by reference to the rent charged.

When you are planning the sale of your pharmacy there are a few other things to consider:

Timing the sale

The point during the year at which you sell your pharmacy will determine when you have to pay the tax on any capital gain that you make. Capital gains tax is payable on January 31 following the end of the tax year in which the gain is made. The tax year ends on April 5, so if you sold your pharmacy on March 31, 2015, the tax would be payable on January 31, 2016. If you deferred the sale to April 30, 2015, the tax would not be payable until January 31, 2017, giving you a cash flow advantage by deferring the tax bill for a year and allowing you to invest the money during this period.

The way in which sales are carried out for sole traders and partnerships usually means that the exchange of contracts occurs prior to completion. For tax purposes the exchange date will normally be the one that determines when your tax liability arises. Make sure that your exchange of contract date is just after the start of the new tax year to gain maximum cash flow advantage.

Overlap relief

Because of the way the tax system works you may have had some profits that were taxed twice when you first started trading. Fortunately there is an allowance for this when the business ceases. This is called Overlap Relief and can be offset against your final business profit when you cease to trade. The objective is to ensure that over the life of the business you do not pay tax on more than the profit you have actually earned. Any overlap profit should have been calculated at the outset of trading, and there is a box on the self-assessment tax return for the amount to be stated and carried forward each year. In many cases this has not been done and consequently when the final business profits are calculated it is overlooked.

If your overlap profit was £10,000 and you pay tax at 40 per cent this would reduce your tax bill by £4,000.

If your overlap profit was £30,000 and you pay tax at 40 per cent this would reduce your tax bill by £12,000.

Apportionment of sale proceeds

Typically the price agreed for the sale of your pharmacy will be for the goodwill, and fixtures and fittings. How should the price be allocated to these items?

If you are entitled to ER it is usually more beneficial to have as much of the sale price as possible allocated to goodwill. The original cost of your fixtures and fittings will probably already have been claimed as a capital allowance with the effect of reducing your trading profit. If an amount of the business sale proceeds is allocated to fixtures and fittings this may result in a balancing charge and thereby increase your income tax liability in your final trading accounts.

John agrees a price of £900,000 for the sale of his business during 2014. He acquired the goodwill in 2001 for £400,000. He is entitled to Entrepreneur's Relief, but for simplicity any expenses or other allowances he may be entitled to will be ignored. During his period of ownership John has spent various amounts on fixtures and fittings, and his accountant has claimed the maximum tax relief available each year under the capital allowances rules. This has left John with £2,000 unclaimed at the time when the business is sold.

If all the sale proceeds are allocated to goodwill John's capital gains tax liability should be approximately £50,000 (£900,000 − £400,000 = £500,000 x10%).

In addition he will have a balancing allowance of the £2,000 previously unclaimed capital allowance which will reduce his final trading profit by £2,000. If he is a 40 per cent taxpayer this will save him £800 tax.

*Therefore John's net tax bill will be £50,000 – £800 = **£49,200***

If, instead, John agrees to apportion the proceeds so that £890,000 is for goodwill and £10,000 for fixtures and fittings his tax position would be higher.

The tax on goodwill would be £49,000 (£890,000 – £400,000 = £490,000 x10%). However, there would be additional tax to pay on the fixtures and fittings as follows:

Capital allowances unclaimed	*£2,000*
Less proceeds from business sale	*£10,000*
Balancing charge	*£8,000*
At 40 per cent tax this would cost John	***£3,200***

Purchasers like to apportion as much as they can to fixtures and fittings as this will qualify for capital allowances in their accounts. You, as the seller, would usually be looking to apportion as much as you can to the goodwill to avoid paying tax on the disposal of the fittings and equipment. The Revenue can challenge apportionments if they think them unreasonable.

VAT

Do you have to pay VAT on the sale of your business? The answer is no, providing it is sold as a going concern, which a pharmacy business normally is.

Can you reclaim the VAT on the fees you incur relating to the sale of the business such as agents' and solicitors' fees. The answer to this is yes. As a sole trader or partnership you can include this on your VAT return as a business expense in the normal way.

Inheritance tax

As inheritance tax applies to a person's estate following their death it is often overlooked when selling a business. If you are a pharmacy owner, and as long as you have owned your pharmacy for at least two years, you should qualify for Business Property Relief should you die while still the owner of the business. This generous provision will exempt your business from inheritance tax. As soon as you sell your business you will, in most cases, no longer be entitled to this relief. Many pharmacists are unaware of this when they sell up, and it is another reason to take professional advice before you do so.

Company sales

If you are trading through a limited company the first thing to consider is what you are actually selling. You have a choice of selling the assets and keeping the company, or selling the whole company.

An asset sale involves selling the pharmacy goodwill, fixtures and fittings, and stock. This will leave you still owning the company. The proceeds of the sale will be paid into the company, and the company will pay corporation tax on the gain. If you want to take the money out of the company you will have to pay tax on it personally. For many people this double taxation can be extremely expensive.

The alternative is to sell the company shares, which means that you sell the whole company including all its assets and liabilities. This route means that you will only pay tax once on the gain made from the sale of your shares.

For the majority of pharmacy owners a share sale will be the best route to minimise any tax liability. However, there can be exceptions, for example, where the company owns other assets such as properties which you don't wish to sell, or you intend to acquire another business in which you can roll over the gain.

The reason why it is more tax efficient for most pharmacists to sell the shares in their company is because it creates a capital gains tax liability. Since most pharmacy owners will qualify for Entrepreneurs' Relief this allows any gains to be taxed at an effective rate of 10 per cent (rather than the standard 28 per cent). There are a number of conditions, which must be met to qualify for ER, which are:

- The shares being sold must be in your personal company, which is one where you own at least 5 per cent of the ordinary shares and voting rights.
- You must also be an officer or employee of the company, and the company must be a trading company, or holding company of a trading group.

The 'trading company' condition is worth further mention because while a pharmacy is a trading concern and you may think your company will qualify for ER, this is not always the case. If the company has substantial other investments or its non-trading assets (for example, property not used in the pharmacy trade) are substantial compared with its total assets, it may not qualify as a trading company. One further qualifying condition for ER is that the business must have been owned for at least one year. The following example illustrates the difference in tax when a share sale qualifies for ER:

James agrees the sale of his company shares, which qualify for ER.

The taxable gain before ER was	£700,000
Capital gains tax payable at 10 per cent	**£70,000**

Susan agrees the sale of her company shares, which do not qualify for ER. Susan is a higher rate tax payer.

The taxable gain is	£700,000

ER Nil

Taxable gain	£700,000
Tax payable at 28 per cent	**£196,000**

If you have recently bought a pharmacy or transferred your sole trader or partnership into a company the qualifying period of one year for ER starts from when you acquired or transferred the business. As the average sale takes around six months from start to finish you could put the business up for sale before the 12 month period has been met.

If you personally own the premises from which the business trades and sell this with the pharmacy the property may qualify for ER. However, it will form part of your lifetime allowance of £10 million. The rules regarding property are complicated and where you have let the property to your company ER relief may be restricted by reference to the rent charged.

If your gains are likely to exceed the £10 million limit for ER you should take advice from a tax expert as soon as possible. There are ways to keep the tax on the sale of your business at 10 per cent, but the analysis and plan of action must usually be carried out more than 12 months before the sale.

Structure of a share sale

Typically when you sell a pharmacy a price will be agreed for the goodwill, and for the fixtures and fittings. In addition, the buyer will expect to purchase the stock. In reality there will be other assets in the company, such as cash and debtors, together with liabilities such as money owed to creditors. An adjustment is therefore made to the share price to take into account the net assets and liabilities.

It is important to negotiate this part of the sale to your best advantage to minimise your tax liability. For example, if you have surplus cash of £100,000 in the company do you take this out by way of a pre-sale dividend or do you add it to the share price? If you qualify for ER it may be more tax efficient to include this in the share price, as the effective tax rate will only be 10 per cent. These issues should be negotiated with your purchaser at the outset before you accept their offer. It is difficult to try and change the terms of the sale after you have accepted the offer.

Taking assets out of the company

You may wish to sell your company but have assets in it that you don't want to include in the sale, such as a car or a property. There is nothing to stop you transferring these assets from the company into your own name, however, beware of the tax consequences. The transfer will be treated as having taken place at market value for tax purposes with tax liabilities for you and possibly the company. If you pay the company full market value for the assets there is no tax issue for you, although there may be a tax liability for the company.

PEG Ltd owns a retail pharmacy business and an investment property which is let out. Patrick, who owns PEG Ltd, decides to sell the pharmacy but wants to keep the investment property to generate future rental income for his retirement.

The property cost £50,000 seven years ago and the market value is now £100,000. Patrick transfers the property into his name and pays the company nothing for it.

The tax position is:

PEG Ltd will be liable to tax on the gain (£100,000 – £50,000) of £50,000 less any allowances it may be entitled to.

Patrick will be treated as having received income from the company (a dividend or salary bonus) of £100,000, which is the market value of the property. The tax on the dividend/bonus will be substantial and there may be more than one tax payable by Patrick, and perhaps his company, depending on how the transfer is organised.

Transferring assets out of a company can be an expensive option as illustrated above. In some cases the assets can be substantial and you may then wish to consider transferring them by means of a hive-up or demerger. Both of these methods are complex but the outcome is to separate out the business assets into a new company (or companies) in a tax efficient way. This then allows you to sell the company with the pharmacy business while retaining the other assets in a separate company. Using either of these methods involves complex procedures shrouded in tax legislation, and requires expert advice.

The issue of removing assets from a company should be addressed before the company is put on the market. In most cases this would need to be completed more than 12 months before the pharmacy is sold in order to qualify for 10 per cent tax on the gain on disposal.

Timing the sale

If you sell the shares in your pharmacy company, the date the sale completes will determine when you have to pay the tax on the capital gain that you make. Capital gains tax, as explained earlier, is payable by January 31 following the end of the tax year in which the gain is made. Deferring a sale until shortly after the start of the tax year means any tax would not be payable until the January following the end of that tax year, giving you a cash flow advantage by deferring the tax bill for up to 21 months.

If you sell the assets and keep the company, the company tax will be payable nine months after your company year end. If the sale is happening close to your company's year end it may be worth delaying it to the start of your new accounting year. If the timing is important to you, make sure your solicitor understands this.

Inheritance tax

As with a sole trader, as long as you have owned your pharmacy company for at least two years, you will probably qualify for Business Property Relief. This will exempt your company from inheritance tax should you die while you still own the business. When you sell your company you will no longer be entitled to this valuable relief in most cases. Many pharmacists are unaware of the implications for them when they sell their business.

John owns a company worth £1 million. If he dies while he still owns the business, in most cases (ie where the company is a qualifying trading business) this will not be taken into account when calculating any inheritance tax on his estate.

John sells the company and puts £1 million in the bank. A week later he is unfortunately killed in an accident. The cash from his business sale will form part of his estate for inheritance tax and potentially the tax liability could be as much as:

£1,000,000 x inheritance tax at 40 per cent = £400,000

This results in the Revenue getting a nice bonus of £400,000. John's heirs would receive £400,000 less than they would have done if John had died a few days earlier while he still owned the business.

Key points for a successful sale

Tax legislation is complicated with many grey areas. You should take professional advice at an early stage regarding your tax position from an expert in tax and business sales.

CHAPTER 5

Choosing the right advisers

Selling a business is complicated. It can take a long time and it can be stressful, and in this respect selling a pharmacy is no different to selling any other type of business. It is may well be the biggest transaction you have ever undertaken, with a substantial amount of money at stake. It does not make sense to try and do it all yourself. Good advice should save you far more than it costs and minimise your stress levels at the same time. The question to consider, then, is not whether you need professional advice, but the type of advice you require and how you go about sourcing it.

Your team should consist of a pharmacy agent (business transfer agent), an accountant or tax adviser, a solicitor and probably an independent financial adviser (IFA).

The pharmacy agent

Whether you are just thinking about it or have committed to sell your pharmacy the first adviser to be contacted is usually a pharmacy agent for the simple reason that the first step is to find out how much your business is worth. A good agent should be able to provide the following services:

- A professional valuation after talking to you confidentially about the business and obtaining enough financial information to allow a thorough appraisal of it.
- Meet with you to discuss your requirements and objectives, and to view the pharmacy and the surrounding area.

- Produce a detailed information pack and sales memorandum to present to prospective buyers.
- Introduce genuine buyers to you with the funding to purchase your business.
- Deal with all the buyers' queries and requests.
- Call in the offers and then negotiate the best price, and terms and conditions of sale.
- Prepare the heads of agreement once the terms of the sale have been agreed and then oversee the sale through to completion, liaising with buyer and seller, and their respective advisers throughout the process.

How do you choose a pharmacy agent?

Should you use a pharmacy agent, a general business transfer agent or another intermediary such as your accountant? Pharmacy is a specialist niche market, particularly with regard to valuations, so you should definitely choose an agent who specialises in the sector, and who knows and understands the market.

There are a number of factors which can guide your decision. Recommendation is always helpful, whether it comes from a trade body like the National Pharmacy Association, or a friend who has recently sold their own business. Perhaps you have used a solicitor in the past who specialises in pharmacy and who may be able to recommend an agent to you?

When you contact an agent it is important that you feel you can trust them and that they understand your requirements. Make sure you understand the agent's fee structure, and terms and conditions. Some agents operate on a 'no sale, no fee' basis, while others have sign-up fees, or fees if they find you a buyer but you don't proceed with the sale. Others may tie you in to a long contract so do scrutinise this carefully.

How much will a pharmacy agent charge me?

I conducted some market research recently which showed the fees charged to sellers ranged from zero to 6 per cent of the sale price (calculated as goodwill, and fixtures and fittings). That's quite a difference from agent to agent, so what is a reasonable charge? The standard fee from well-known and respected pharmacy agents who act for you, the vendor, is around 3 per cent but negotiable on large sales. The key is that the agent is acting solely for you and not for the buyer. There are agents who will take fees from both buyers and sellers, and some who just take fees from buyers because that is who they are acting for.

The zero agents are those who say they do not charge you, the seller. These agents make their money by charging the buyer they introduce to you. If the buyer is paying the agent then that is who the agent is acting for. This is the worst scenario for you as a seller, since the agent will be looking for the best deal for their client, the buyer. In this situation no one is looking after your interests.

The amount that a buyer pays such an agent will come out of the overall budget which they have for buying your pharmacy. In other words, if the buyer's budget is £1 million and they have to pay agent's fees of £30,000, the maximum amount that they can offer you will be £970,000. Please don't think that you are saving on agent's fees by going down this route.

Low commission agents charge a small percentage of the sale price, so again you have to ask where their full fee is coming from. If an agent offers to sell your business for 1 per cent, it is likely that the rest of their fee is coming from the buyer. This is a situation for you, as a seller, to avoid because the agent has a conflict of interest and is not acting solely for you in your best interests.

The high commission agents, and the highest I came across charged 6 per cent, are asking for a fee which, for the pharmacy market, is on the high side.

The agent who is going to get you the best price is the one who:

- Is acting for you and not the buyer. This is important: you need someone who is going to put 100 per cent into getting you the best possible price and terms of sale.

- Comes recommended by other pharmacy owners who have sold through them. Ask for testimonials from pharmacists who have sold through the agent.
- Has proper office back-up. When I conducted my market research many of the agents contacted either didn't answer the phone or were on voice mail. On occasions I had to call several times before I was able to speak to someone. A one man band who is difficult to contact is not the agent you want when selling your business.
- Is an active agent who specialises in pharmacy sales. Agents who are in regular contact with the buyers in the market know who the genuine players are, their motivation for acquiring the business and their ability to pay for it.
- Understands the tax implications of your sale. Negotiating the sale with the buyer in the most tax efficient way can save you a lot of money – or cost you a lot if it's not done properly. Don't assume your accountant can do it: most accountants have little experience of pharmacy sales.

Accountant/tax adviser

Your natural instinct may be to ask your existing accountant to handle the accounting and tax issues arising from the sale of your business. The reality is that most firms of accountants, unless they are substantial in size, don't have much experience of dealing with business sales, let alone pharmacy sales which are highly specialised. Time and time again I have seen pharmacy sellers receiving poor and downright costly advice from their accountants. Sadly many accountants would rather give poor advice than admit that they don't have the expertise to handle the complex issues relating to a pharmacy sale.

A pharmacy expert accountant and tax adviser should be able to conduct a pre-sale tax planning review, and provide ongoing advice on:

- Ownership of the business.
- How to minimise capital gains tax payable on the sale.
- How to extract cash in the most tax efficient way.
- Business restructuring where a straightforward sale is difficult or impossible.
- Improving turnover and gross profit in the period leading up to the sale.
- Presenting your accounts in a way which is appealing to potential buyers: this can make a difference to the level of offers you receive.
- Preparing management accounts to improve the sale price of your business, with expenditure analysed in a format which presents your business in the most advantageous way to buyers.
- Calculating all the balance sheet adjustments applicable to company share sales.
- Capital allowances and fixtures and fittings apportionments for sole traders and partnerships to minimise your tax liabilities.
- Reviewing and amending the tax section of the sale contract with buyers to ensure your interests are fully protected.

What are your options if your accountant does not have the expertise to handle the accountancy and tax issues relating to your sale? You could do nothing and hope for the best, although I wouldn't recommend it – it could be very costly for you! If you are not yet convinced let me give you some examples:

I was recently involved in the sale of a small pharmacy group where the owner was advised by his accountant that the business should be sold as an asset sale rather than as a company share sale.

I was surprised by this advice and questioned it. The reason why the accountant told his client to pursue an asset sale was because he thought buyer wouldn't be prepared to buy the company shares. This lack of knowledge could have cost his client £200,000 in tax if I hadn't told the accountant that the sale could be structured as a company share sale

I have lost count of the number of times I have had to assist accountants who do not have the knowledge or experience to handle the calculations of the assets and liabilities at completion of the sale. This is a problem because if the buyer has an accountant who is on the ball they can run rings around the seller and their accountant, meaning the seller receives less money on completion than they would have done if they had received proper advice.

There are accountants who tell their clients to take substantial dividends prior to a company sale when the withdrawal of the cash could be done in a much more tax efficient way.

You could appoint an agent who has the accountancy and tax expertise in-house, and who can either work with your existing accountant or take over completely when required. If you have selected an agent to handle the sale and they can also provide the tax and accountancy services in-house, then having everything under one roof is probably a good option.

You could retain your existing accountant on the understanding that you will appoint another firm with expertise in pharmacy sales to advise you on the tax structure and accountancy issues relating to the sale. This firm can work with your existing accountant, leaving them to do the compliance work such as accounts preparation and your tax returns. Let the two firms work together to achieve the best outcome for you.

Recommendations from other pharmacy owners are a good way of finding an accountant who can handle the issues relating to the sale. However, check that the person making the recommendation has used the accountant for the same type of work that you require them for. If you have already selected an agent they may be able to recommend someone, or a body like the NPA may be able to suggest someone. Once you have a shortlist of firms to contact, prepare an initial list of questions to discuss with them. As a guide you might ask them:

- To what extent do they specialise in pharmacies?
- How many community pharmacies do they act for, and what is the average size of those businesses?
- How many pharmacy sales have they been involved with in the last two years, and in what capacity were they acting?
- What is the extent of the services they provide? Are they able to provide tax planning advice on the sale of a business, including how to structure the sale to minimise any tax?
- How quickly do they respond to calls, e-mails and correspondence?
- How will their fees be charged (you might like a fixed fee for each piece of work discussed, for example)?
- Could they give you an estimate over the telephone and then confirm the fees in writing?

How much will the accountancy and tax services cost?

The cost of tax and accountancy services will vary depending on the amount of work involved. I would recommend that you obtain fixed fees wherever possible since this will make it easier to budget and there should be no nasty surprises. As a rough guide you should budget for additional fees of between £2,000-£5,000 for a sole trader/partnership and £5,000-£10,000 for a single pharmacy company sale

Solicitors

It is a good idea to instruct a solicitor at the outset because legal points often arise early in the sale process. The most important point is to find someone who is familiar with pharmacy sales. In the long run this will save you money as choosing a solicitor who does not have the necessary experience will extend the sale and ultimately end up costing you more. Delays cause frustration and extra stress for both the seller and the buyer. The longer a sale goes on the more likely it is to fall through, so it is in everyone's interest for it to complete in a timely manner.

Your solicitor will be advising you on:

- The sale and purchase contract, which will often contain clauses that are pharmacy specific, such as provisions relating to Category M clawback, information relating to prescription items, and conditions relating to transfer of ownership. If you have a solicitor without pharmacy expertise they will struggle with these issues, and if the buyer's solicitor knows their stuff you will be at a disadvantage.
- Due diligence and warranties, which allow a buyer to make a claim against you under certain circumstances after the sale has been completed.
- Property transfer, whether leasehold or freehold. Having a solicitor who understands lenders' and buyers' requirements when dealing with the drawing up of leases and transfers of leases is important.

How to find a solicitor

Recommendation from other pharmacy owners is a good way to find a solicitor, but check that they have worked on pharmacy sales before. If you are using an agent they should have a list of solicitors who they deal with regularly and are happy to recommend. Before deciding which solicitor to appoint call them and ask questions such as:

- Is your main area of expertise in corporate transactions such as buying and selling businesses, or do you actually specialise in pharmacy transactions?
- Do you deal with many pharmacy owners who are selling pharmacies?
- Are your clients usually just selling goodwill or their whole company?
- Do you deal with many transactions relating to leasehold or freehold business premises?
- If you are not available, what back-up is provided? Would I be able to deal with another experienced solicitor in your firm?

- How long would you estimate the pharmacy sale will take, assuming everything is straightforward?
- How quickly will your firm respond to telephone calls, e-mails and correspondence?
- How will your fees be charged? Is it possible to agree a fixed fee with you? I would like all costs such as expenses and disbursements included in the estimate. Can you let me have an estimate now over the telephone and then confirm it in writing?

How much will the legal services cost?

Solicitor's fees will vary depending on the amount of work involved. As with your accountant I would always recommend you obtain fixed fees wherever possible. As a rough guide you should budget for fees of between £5,000-£10,000 for a sole trader/partnership and £10,000-£20,000 for a single pharmacy company sale.

Independent financial advisors (IFA)

To complete your team of advisors you may want to include an independent financial advisor. Typically you may wish to consult your IFA at the outset to calculate if the sale will provide you with sufficient money to fund your future needs.

If you don't already have an IFA the best way to find someone is, as always, by recommendation from other business owners or high net worth colleagues. If you already have an IFA, make sure that they are still competent to advise you after your circumstances have changed. When the pharmacy has been sold you may require investment advice if you have a large lump sum to invest. Can your IFA provide this?

As with other advisers, when you have a list of candidates draft a list of questions to ask them – and don't forget to ascertain their charging structure!

Finally, it is worth mentioning that once you start appointing professional advisers you will need to provide them with proof of identity to comply with government money laundering regulations.

Key points for a successful sale

1. Surround yourself with the best team of advisers you can find.

2. Good professional advice should make you more money than it costs.

3. Buyers who are aware that you have industry experts acting for you will regard you with more respect and know that you mean business.

CHAPTER 6

Should I sell to a private buyer?

If you own a pharmacy it would be surprising if you haven't been approached by one or more private buyers. Some buyers regularly send out bulk mailings expressing their interest in acquiring 'your pharmacy': just be aware that similar letters will have been received by hundreds of other owners. You may also have been approached by your locum, a local pharmacy owner or perhaps the buying group that you belong to.

It can be flattering when someone tells you what a wonderful business you have, and asks if you would consider selling it. Your years of hard work, sweat and tears have finally been recognised! If you know the individual you may feel an element of trust, and perhaps even a desire to sell to them. That's understandable, but if you are serious about selling hand it over to a professional to negotiate for you. The best way of dealing with private sales is to appoint an agent and include the private buyer in the loop with other buyers who may be introduced to you. This way you can be confident that you are obtaining the full market value for your pharmacy.

When I have included a vendor's private buyer on my circulation list, in 90 per cent of the cases I have ended up selling to a third party who has offered significantly more than the private buyer. In the few cases where the private buyer has purchased the pharmacy, it has been at a much higher price than they had offered initially.

I once sold a pharmacy in Bristol. The pharmacy owner had been in discussions with a private buyer, and contacted me for advice. I suggested that he let me put his pharmacy on the market to get him the top price, and said that I would include his private buyer in the loop. After marketing the business I received five offers. The top offer, which was accepted, was 94 per cent higher than that made by the private buyer.

I have seen many privately arranged sales go wrong, wasting huge amounts of time and causing untold stress, not to mention the pharmacy being sold at far less than its true market value. Private sellers tend to contact me when their sale has gone off the rails, or to ask for an opinion on what the business is worth and whether the price they have been offered is good one. I therefore see the mistakes pharmacists make when they negotiate their own sale.

The seller's experience

So what can sellers experience when they try and sell their pharmacy themselves? Perhaps I only hear about the ones that go wrong but from the number of pharmacists who contact me it seems that an awful lot of private sales do go belly up. If you are selling your business it is likely that you have no previous experience to guide you. You don't really want to be on a learning curve and making mistakes with what is likely to be the most valuable asset you have.

A pharmacist contacted me because he had been trying to sell his business privately for nearly four years, and there was still no end in sight! He did not know what to do next.

First a multiple had approached him and the sale had been agreed only for the multiple to pull out. Then an agent contacted him on behalf of a specific buyer. (Remember, when an agent brings a buyer to you in this way, the agent will be acting for the buyer and not you). Again the sale was agreed, and again it fell through.

Next a private buyer contacted him and again a sale was agreed. The sale had been dragging on for months when the seller contacted me. In fact, it had been due to complete over six months earlier but the buyer was dragging the sale on and on. During this time the buyer had managed to renegotiate a reduced price from what was already a low price of about £300,000 to £400,000 under the proper market value. In addition the buyer changed other previously agreed terms which made the deal more expensive in terms of tax for the seller. Even after the seller had caved in to these unreasonable demands there was still no completion date on the horizon!

The seller had got to the point where his focus was almost entirely on the sale to the detriment of his business. It wasn't surprising that the seller told me that selling his business on his own was something he would never want to do again.

Underselling the business

The only way you can be sure of obtaining the best price for your pharmacy is by getting competitive offers from different buyers. If you are only talking to a single private buyer they know that they have the upper hand in terms of negotiating the price, and terms and conditions of the sale. Why would they offer more than they need to?

The table below demonstrates examples of uplifts in offers I have received on a few recent pharmacy sales.

Location	Lowest offer	Highest offer	Uplift	% Uplift
Essex	£2,950,000	£3,500,000	£550,000	19%
N. London	£1,000,000	£1,310,000	£310,000	31%
Scotland	£571,000	£675,000	£104,000	18%
South Wales	£2,600,000	£3,200,000	£600,000	23%
Northampton	£700,000	£1,000,000	£300,000	43%

This illustrates the importance of having a number of offers. If you are selling privately and dealing with one buyer you are likely to achieve close to the lowest offer. The objective should always be to generate interest and competition for the pharmacy, resulting in several offers, which then paves the way to negotiating the top price.

Breach of confidentiality

For most pharmacy owners maintaining confidentiality is one of their biggest worries during the sale of their business. If you are trying to deal with the sale yourself you may find it difficult to maintain confidentiality, as you will be dealing with the whole process yourself. This involves not just dealing with potential buyers but also their advisers as well as your own. This can be time consuming and it won't be long before your staff guess what is going on.

Buyers who can't fund the purchase

A high percentage of sales fall through because the buyer cannot raise sufficient funds to buy the business. When a buyer makes an offer for your business how can you know if they really have the money? Naturally they will say they have got funding, and may genuinely believe that this is the case. The problem is that people often have little idea of the true costs involved in buying a business, particularly inexperienced first time buyers who have not been through the process before. The reality is that many of these buyers will fall down on the financing and be unable to complete. You are unlikely to find this out until you are a few months down the line, having invested time and money progressing the sale.

Remember, anyone can make an offer on your business, but an offer without financial backing is worthless. A good pharmacy agent will be dealing with buyers every day and will know how much pharmacists can realistically borrow, and their sources of funding: put simply an agent should know whether a buyer is going to be able to finance the purchase of your pharmacy. They should also require proof of funds and check that the buyer has some contingency to cover the likely scenario of their lender valuing the pharmacy at less than the agreed price.

Time wasters

If you are dealing with pharmacy sales day in, day out, you soon get to know the credible buyers and come to recognise the time wasters. There is the potential buyer who falls into the category of what I call a 'paper trader': they go through the motions but never actually commit any money. This type of buyer can take up a lot of your time while never progressing to completion. They will get cold feet somewhere along the line and the sale will disintegrate. Another type of 'buyer' to beware of is the 'dipper', who is fishing for information about your business. They may just be curious about how you are doing, or they may be a local competitor who is looking to take some of your business and wants to see your figures so that they can calculate the potential for improving their own.

An important part of an agent's job is to put together deals which have a realistic expectation of completion. There are plenty of buyers out there who do have the commitment and ability to purchase. The key is knowing who they are.

Buyers who use the private sale to their advantage

There are some large players in the market who seem to change the way they operate when negotiating a private deal. Suddenly, shortly before completion, they decide to reduce the price, try to re-negotiate previously agreed terms, or maybe pull out completely on some flimsy pretext.

These buyers try to take advantage of the private sale situation which they have engineered, knowing that the seller has nobody advising them or looking after their interests. I believe such buyers behave differently when dealing directly with the vendor in a private sale because they know that if a seller has gone through an agent there will be other buyers lined up. If the original buyer drops out the agent can go to the next on the list.

If a group is regularly acquiring pharmacies it needs to build up a relationship with pharmacy agents otherwise it will cut itself off from a large part of the market. If a group builds a bad reputation for itself agents aren't going to want to deal with it or recommend it to their clients.

Just because a large group makes an offer for your pharmacy it doesn't necessarily mean it's a good one or that the deal will actually complete. Again it's all about knowing the market.

Poor terms of sale

Selling a pharmacy can be complicated. There will be many issues that have to be agreed with the buyer, not least being the structure of the sale. I often get called by private sellers who have agreed a sale and then have concerns over whether they should be getting a higher price for their business. The answer to that is often 'yes', but time and time again when I delve into what has actually been agreed I find that the buyer has also insisted on a structure which suits them and will result in the seller paying thousands more in tax than they need to.

Most sellers have little idea of the financial consequences of what they have agreed to, or how they should have negotiated the sale to their benefit. Sadly, the seller's accountant often doesn't have the knowledge or experience of pharmacy sales to guide or help their client achieve the best outcome.

> *In a recent case I was involved in the seller's accountant had not only completely misunderstood how to structure the deal, but to make matters worse, kept on insisting he was right!*
>
> *The seller eventually realised he was not getting proper advice and asked me for help. After negotiating with the buyer and their lender I was able to structure the sale so that the seller saved £80,000 in tax.*

There are many other points which arise during a sale. Listed below are a few areas you need to keep an eye on:

- *Stock* The buyer may not want to purchase all the stock. Would you know what the normal stock level was for your pharmacy and how to negotiate on this?
- *Retentions* Buyers often propose they retain part of the sale proceeds for a period of time as contingency. Would you know what was acceptable in the pharmacy market and how to negotiate this?
- *Re-negotiation during the sale* There can be many reasons why a buyer may try to renegotiate after a sale has been agreed. These might include a Category M announcement, the loss of business from a care home, or your latest NHS FP34 statements may show a drop in prescription items, to name but a few. Would you be able to assess these situations, and know whether the buyer was trying it on, or if there was a sufficient loss of value in the business to warrant a price reduction? Renegotiation is a common problem in private sales.

Why do it yourself?

Why do some pharmacy owners try and sell their business themselves? Sometimes it can look like an easy option to sell to someone who you know like your locum, or a pharmacy group or agent who has contacted you directly. Unfortunately, with no competition these buyers are unlikely to offer you the top price or best terms and conditions. If you have someone you particularly want to sell your pharmacy to, it is still worth engaging an agent to handle the negotiations for you. You will have to pay the agent's fee, but that should be far less than the additional price obtained. If you are concerned about this, negotiate an agreement with the agent where they will only be paid if the price they negotiate exceeds that which you have agreed privately.

Comments made by a client in Yorkshire after I sold his group of pharmacies:

"I contacted you as I had been struggling with what was being offered privately by the buyer and his advisers and the structure of the sale, and found it overwhelming.

"You took all the issues on board, vetted the buyer to ensure sufficient funds were available, re-negotiated the deal and improved the terms and conditions, which resulted in you securing a substantial deposit from the buyer as well as negotiating a higher price than was originally offered."

If you are selling the business yourself you will be starting from a position of weakness if this is not your area of expertise. A buyer will use the situation to their advantage in negotiating as low a price as they can, and terms and conditions to suit them. As the business is not on the open market the buyer also knows that they will be in a strong position during the process of the sale to try and renegotiate the price.

Some pharmacists see dealing with the sale themselves as a new challenge. The risk is that in focusing on the sale, which will be time consuming and stressful, you will not be looking after your business properly. If you switch focus away from your pharmacy then the business is likely to deteriorate, and reduced turnover and profits means reduced goodwill value.

Key points for a successful sale

1. Don't be tempted to try and take short cuts by selling to someone who approaches you privately.

2. A good pharmacy agent should obtain more offers for you and at a higher price than you could achieve yourself.

CHAPTER 7

Information for the sale

Before you can sell your business you need to provide comprehensive documentation to your prospective buyer and their advisers. Often the required information I ask for is sadly lacking: the accounts are out of date, NHS statements are missing, and VAT returns are incorrectly prepared. You cannot seriously expect to sell your business without proper information. Would you buy a pharmacy from someone who couldn't provide the basic financial information to support the price they are asking?

If you are fortunate enough to find someone who tells you that they will buy the business with documentation missing you are still likely to encounter problems. The buyer may well offer a reduced price because of the uncertainty created. In the pharmacy market most buyers will not be interested in a poorly presented and documented business, so if someone is prepared to proceed they will be in a good position to acquire your pharmacy at a knock down price.

The buyer's advisers will not be happy with the situation either. If the buyer tries to get bank finance for the acquisition they will hit a brick wall. Banks are cautious these days, even when all the paperwork is in place! It is likely that the sale will fall through at this stage, or the buyer will come back with an even lower offer.

> One unusual 'missing information' case I dealt with recently involved a pharmacist who had not submitted his NHS monthly reimbursement claims for over a year. This was quite bizarre! How he thought we were going to be able to sell the business with no idea what his income should have been for the past year, I don't know!

If you wish to get the maximum price for your pharmacy you must be thorough with your preparation. Collecting the required information can be split into three stages.

Stage 1 – Initial valuation and appraisal of the business

Once you start to think about selling your pharmacy the first thing to do is to obtain a valuation for the goodwill. This is the main asset of your business, and if you know what it is worth it will help you to decide if the time is right to sell. For an initial valuation and appraisal I would require the following information:

- Accounts for the past year, and sometimes for the past three years, depending on the circumstances.
- VAT returns for the past 12 months. If these have been correctly completed Box 6 will give the total turnover figure, providing the turnover of the business for the past 12 months.
- NHS statements for the past 12 months, from which it can be seen whether the NHS income is going up or down.

Additional information that I would ask for includes:

- A summary of the counter trade for the past 12 months, excluding VAT but including NHS levies if applicable. Again, this gives an indication of how the counter trade is performing when compared with the earlier years.
- Details of any other income received by the pharmacy in the past 12 months which has not been covered. For example, some NHS services may be paid for separately, or the business may have income from letting spare rooms in the premises to other health professionals.
- Details of any income from wholesaling and internet sales if applicable. This is important since, as noted earlier, buyers won't generally pay for wholesaling, and the small gross

margin will dilute the overall gross margin for your main pharmacy business. You need to be able to separate out any wholesaling income for the purpose of valuation. Internet sales also need to be reviewed carefully.

- A staff list, their roles, their hours per week and hourly rate of pay, plus details of any locum hours and rates of pay. Many pharmacies are overstaffed or paying salaries that are higher than average, so it is important to review staff costs and, if appropriate, see where savings could be made.

- Details of any residential or nursing homes you deal with. This should include the number of homes and the monthly prescription volume they generate. If it accounts for more than 10 per cent of your turnover it will impact the goodwill value.

- Percentage of items supplied in monitored dosage systems. If this makes up more than 10 per cent of turnover the time involved in servicing these patients needs to be considered.

- The number of drug addicts you deal with. Large numbers will have a positive effect on the gross margin, but on the negative side not every buyer is keen on business from this source.

- Details of your lease or, if you own the freehold, the market rent for the premises and its approximate size (property issues are covered in detail in Chapter 8).

- Details of anything you are aware of which could affect the value of the business, either positively or negatively. The more positive things the better, since these can be emphasised to buyers in the marketing process and will make the business more attractive. It is also important to be aware of negatives. Buyers will do their due diligence and it is better to be realistic at the outset about something that may affect the value of the pharmacy.

- The location of nearby GP surgeries or health centres, and the percentage of prescription items that come from your main surgery.

- Information on your main competitors and the approximate distance they are from your premises.
- The potential for growing the business, since pharmacies with potential to grow are more popular with buyers and will fetch a higher price.
- The opening hours of the pharmacy. Pharmacies with long hours which are located outside London are not so popular with buyers.
- Whether the business has been on the market in the last few years, and if so a brief history of the circumstances including details of any offers which may have been received. If the pharmacy has been on the market before buyers are likely to be aware of this and will want to know why it didn't sell.

This is a long list but if you want a proper valuation this is the sort of information a valuer should be asking for. All these points have relevance and are important when assessing the likely outcome of the sale. If the valuer genuinely understands the pharmacy market they will be looking at the bottom line profitability of the business plus the premium that a buyer will pay. If you speak to someone who just asks a couple of questions and then gives you a valuation, take it with a pinch of salt!

What happens next if, following the valuation, you decide to sell? You will need to provide sufficient information to prospective buyers to enable them to make an offer for your business. Before you do that you may wish to ask them to sign a confidentiality agreement (there is a sample confidentiality agreement in Chapter 9).

The purpose of a confidentiality agreement is to stop any prospective buyers from disclosing that your pharmacy is for sale, and to prevent them from disclosing the information they receive to anyone other than their financial advisers. This can be important because you probably don't want your staff or the local community to be aware of the sale at this early stage. In reality it will probably be difficult to enforce one of these agreements but they do serve as a reminder that confidentiality is a serious issue. Any buyer that breaches such an agreement is not likely to be viewed favourably.

Stage 2 – Documents required for marketing the business

The good news is that you have already collated most of the necessary documentation you need for the initial valuation. Additional information required at this stage is likely to include:

- A further 12 months of NHS statements, counter trade figures and VAT returns, so that in total 24 months of paperwork is available. Be aware that buyers are likely to request full NHS statements, not just the first page.
- Accounts for the past three years. Since you have already produced accounts for the previous year, you will only need to produce figures for another two years.
- A copy of your pharmacy leaflet(s).

On occasion buyers may request more information, for example, wholesaler statements, so it pays to gather together as much information as possible in the first instance. However, figures going back three years should be enough. One way of building trust with buyers and giving them confidence in the business is to provide a detailed and up-to-date information pack.

I cannot emphasise enough the importance of making sure that your accounts are up-to-date. Although the NHS statements and other supporting data should give a good picture of the pharmacy's income, buyers and their advisers expect to see the latest accounts before making any offers. In one recent sale I dealt with the accounts took around 10 weeks to come through from the seller's accountant. As a result momentum was lost and some of the prospective buyers lost interest in the sale altogether. This undoubtedly had a negative effect on the price the seller got for the business.

Still on the topic of accounts, make sure they are correct! Buyers can lose trust in the information provided and the sale can be jeopardised if they examine the figures and find anomalies, or if your accountant notices mistakes and makes amendments.

I had a case recently where the sale had been agreed based on the accounts provided, and was close to completion. The latest accounts were produced with comparative figures for the previous year. However, these comparative figures were different (less turnover and profits) from those shown in the original accounts.

As the sale had been agreed based on the original accounts for the previous year the buyer and his solicitor were upset and lost faith in the deal. It turned out that the vendor had changed his accountant. The new accountant, who did not fully understand how to account for NHS income, had recalculated the income for that year and missed out an NHS payment from the accounts.

Fortunately I was able to resolve the situation and get the sale back on track for completion, but it was a close call.

Stage 3 – Documents required by your solicitor and your buyer's advisers

When you have agreed the sale with your buyer the final stage is completing the legal process and this is where a further swathe of documentation is required. This will include:

- Contracts of employment, payroll records, sickness records, staff bonuses and staff training details. Sometimes buyers will ask for additional information such as staff dates of birth as this will give them an idea of when people are likely to retire. They will also want details of any staff contracts that are to be terminated prior to completion of the sale, including any compromise agreements.
- Details of any pensions or life assurance schemes offered

to employees through the business, since this could have a major impact on costs.

- Copies of any handbooks and procedures used by the business.
- If you operate through a company, minutes of director and shareholder meetings, and the company's articles of association.
- For company sales, copies of corporation tax returns plus details of any recent or ongoing HMRC investigations. Buyers will also require details of HMRC clearances and tax elections.
- All insurance documents and details of imminent or ongoing claims.
- Details of any litigation or pending litigation.
- Details of any complaints, investigations and inspections.
- Copy of title deed or lease for pharmacy premises.
- An Energy Performance Certificate for the premises.
- Asbestos survey/fire health check.
- HN1 form showing core and supplementary hours.
- Details of the pharmacy's registration with the General Pharmaceutical Council and any supporting documentation.
- Recent stock valuation.
- Details of any collection/delivery arrangements with local surgeries.
- Details of your principal wholesaler.
- Recent invoices for rates, and services such as water, gas, electricity and telephone.
- All hire purchase, rental, and lease agreements.
- A list of assets, eg computers, equipment, fixtures, fittings and vehicles owned by the business and to be included in the sale.
- Copies of any permits or licences.
- Copies of any guarantees or indemnities affecting the business.
- Details of any long term contracts or commitments.
- Details of any loans or mortgages attached to the business.
- Maintenance, support and service agreements for computers, equipment, waste and disposal.

- Details of changes or notifications for inclusion in Pharmaceutical List in the past 12 months.
- Details of any LIFT schemes or changes to GP surgeries.

This is by no means an exhaustive list but gives a good indication of the information that you need to pull together to pass onto your solicitor. The choice is whether to collate the documents one stage at a time, or whether to take a day or two out from the pharmacy and dedicate the time to putting all this information together in one go.

Key points for a successful sale

1. Have a good look at your business through the eyes of a buyer. Can you see areas that concern you? If so they will also be of concern to a buyer so try and address them before putting the pharmacy on the market.

2. Get your accounts up to date before putting the business on the market and make sure you have all the other information you will need readily available.

CHAPTER 8

Freehold and leasehold property issues

The premises you trade from are a vital element when it comes to selling your pharmacy. Your buyer and their lenders will need to be satisfied that the business has security of tenure on a long term basis. While it may be possible to relocate locally, numerous conditions have to be met and suitable premises found. Without security of tenure it can be virtually impossible to sell a pharmacy.

One of the first things I discuss with pharmacy sellers is the type of property they have: do they own the freehold or lease the premises? This chapter looks at some of the issues relating to freehold ownership and leasehold tenancies.

Freehold premises

If you own the freehold for your business premises the first question to ask yourself is whether you want to sell it, and if so will a buyer wish to acquire it? Some people decide to keep the freehold as the rent from it will provide them with a future income. If this applies to you, do you own the property personally or through the limited company that also owns your pharmacy? If you are trading through a company and you intend to sell that company you will need to remove the property first if you are going to retain ownership of it. There are tax implications in doing this, so make sure you take good tax advice at the outset.

You may wish to sell the premises with the pharmacy. In most cases this can work well, however there are limits on what buyers are prepared to pay for the property freehold. In my experience where a property is worth more than a few hundred thousand pounds buyers become reluctant to part with their money. If the pharmacy is aimed at first time buyers they do not normally have the resources to purchase a high value freehold.

> *In a recent sale I had a pharmacy on the books with goodwill of around £350,000 and a freehold of approximately £500,000. The pharmacy owner was adamant that the freehold had to be sold. This was really a first time buyer's pharmacy but they just couldn't afford the freehold. I eventually found an existing pharmacy owner who was willing to take the freehold with the pharmacy at a slightly reduced price.*

If your freehold is worth up to about £300,000 it is usually quite easy to sell. Occasionally the buyer may want to buy the property but doesn't have the additional funds after paying for the pharmacy business. In such a situation you may decide to give them the option to purchase the premises within the next five years at market value or, to give you more flexibility, you may decide to offer them 'first refusal' if you sell in the future.

Whether you decide to lease or sell your freehold, the first step is to have a professional valuation carried out by a commercial surveyor. It is worth using someone with local knowledge as they will know the area well and give a true market value for your particular location. I always recommend that you ask the surveyor to give you figures for both market rent and freehold value. This leaves your options open: although your preference may be to lease the property, if the buyer makes you an offer you can't refuse you may decide to sell the freehold. I have had cases where a premium price has been negotiated on a freehold which the vendor didn't really want to sell but the buyer was desperate to acquire.

You should expect the buyer to have their own valuation of the freehold carried out along with a structural survey. If they find dilapidations expect them to negotiate on the price! I suggest that when you instruct your surveyor to value the property you ask them to give a figure at the top of the range for both the freehold valuation and the market rent as this leaves room for negotiation.

There are circumstances where you might not use a local surveyor, particularly for health centre pharmacies where different methods of valuation can apply. If you own a health centre premises and intend to create a lease for your buyer I recommend that you consult an expert in this area because health centre rents are usually charged at a premium. The rent often bears no resemblance to local commercial 'pound per square foot' calculation and can vary widely. Often it will be based on the total prescription item output from the GPs in the health centre, but there are other factors that can – and should – be considered. Ultimately there is no hard and fast rule for establishing a rent level for pharmacy tenants inside a health centre. A lot will come down to negotiation, but in 99 per cent of cases a higher rent will be agreed to allow a pharmacy to occupy such a priority location.

Some freehold premises comprise the shop floor with accommodation or storage on the floors above. To maximise the value of the premises it may be worth developing the accommodation. Could you convert the space into flats subject, of course, to planning consent? This could enhance the value of the property, but be aware that the flat(s) will need a separate entrance from the pharmacy and separate utilities.

Make sure you have all relevant property documentation available at the outset of the sale process to avoid unnecessary delays and problems later.

> *I recall one particular case where the sale was almost at completion when it came to light that the vendor had misplaced the title deeds to the premises. The sale with the existing buyer broke down as a result since the bank would not support the purchase without the document. I successfully found another purchaser whose solicitor was able to find a way around the problem and the deal was finally completed!*

Setting up a lease

If you decide to keep your freehold and set up a lease, instruct a good property solicitor who will advise you on the various clauses. These are a few of the main points to consider:

Length of the lease The buyer of your pharmacy, who will become your tenant, will require a lease under the Landlord and Tenant Act 1954. This means that, with a few exceptions such as you wanting the property back for your own use or if you intend to develop the premises, the tenant will be able to renew the lease at the end of the term. The tenant will require a minimum period of 10 years on the lease, although sometimes lenders will ask for a longer period to correspond with the term of the buyer's loan. It is not unusual for leases to be for 15 or 20 years.

Break clause It is common for a tenant to request a break clause in the lease. The reason for this is that if there is a development in the locality which could have a detrimental effect on the pharmacy, the owner does not want to be tied into a long lease which may prevent the business from relocating. A typical scenario is where the local GP surgery moves and it makes sense to relocate the pharmacy to be near to the new surgery. Break clauses can be negotiated around whatever suits you and the tenant, for example every five years or, if the tenant's main concern is a surgery relocation, you could agree to a break clause just to cover that one situation.

Rent reviews These are usually every three, four or five years. I suggest that you start from three years and then be prepared to negotiate. There is usually a provision for upwards only rent reviews. At the review date the rent is reassessed at open market rates or possibly against an indexation formula.

Repairs and maintenance It is usually the tenant's responsibility to maintain the property to a good standard. Don't be surprised if the tenant has a survey carried out before they sign the lease so that any major work required can be established as your liability rather than your tenant's responsibility.

Rent payment The lease will contain provision for how the rent is to be paid – monthly or quarterly.

Use of the premises The lease will usually say what type of trade can be carried out from the premises and possibly what goods can be sold. From a tenant's perspective the more flexible this is the better because if circumstances change and the pharmacy relocates to other premises the tenant may wish to sublet the original premises. If the lease says that only a pharmacy business can be carried out this could be a problem!

Alterations The lease usually includes restrictions on what alterations can be made and may require the landlord's consent before any work can be carried out.

Subletting or assigning the lease If your tenant no longer uses the premises for a pharmacy business – perhaps they cease to trade or relocate the pharmacy – they may wish to sublet the premises or assign the lease to a new tenant. If they sublet they remain as tenant while granting a sub-lease to a third party. A lease assignment is where a new tenant takes over the existing lease in its entirety. Similarly, if your tenant sells the pharmacy the new owner will wish to take on the lease. Usually there will be a clause saying that landlord's consent (not to be unreasonably withheld) is required.

Other payments The lease will specify who is liable for what. For example, the landlord may insure the buildings but the tenant may be liable for all the utility bills and the rates.

Breach of terms The lease will contain provisions for situations where the tenant is in breach of the terms in the lease or becomes insolvent.

I had a situation where, unbeknown to me, a vendor was in difficulty with the rent payments on his premises. By the time he informed me of the problem and how serious it was the landlord had already, under the provisions in the lease, revoked the lease and changed the locks!

After discussing the situation with the landlord, he commented that if he had spoken to me sooner and been made aware that the matter was being dealt with professionally; he may not have revoked the lease at all. With the pharmacy owner having no trading premises, administrators were brought in and offers for the business were subsequently significantly reduced.

Whether you are selling the freehold of the property or intending to set up a lease for the buyer of the business you will need to obtain an Energy Performance Certificate (EPC). The exception to this is where the property is owned by the company which you are selling. For example, you do not need to produce an EPC if the pharmacy goodwill and premises are owned by your company and you are selling the whole company. In other circumstances where, for example, you are retaining the property and creating a lease or you personally own the property and are selling it, you will require an EPC.

Leasehold premises

If your pharmacy premises are leasehold you should check whether or not the lease is held under the Landlord and Tenant Act 1954. If it is not, how long does the lease have left to run? If it is less than 10 years it will be difficult to sell the business, and if you do find a buyer it will be at a much reduced price. In these circumstances you should try and renew the lease with your landlord and have it included under the Landlord and Tenant Act. There are circumstances where you may need to pay the landlord a premium to obtain a lease that will enable you to sell your business.

I was once asked to sell a health centre pharmacy in the Midlands.

The lease only had a few years left to run, and was not under the Landlord and Tenant Act. Even though the buyers were prepared to take some risk their bank would not lend them the funds.

The problem was that when that lease expired the pharmacy owner would have no security of tenure. This meant they could be asked to leave or, more likely, the landlord would demand a huge premium and rent increase to create a new lease. This uncertainty and risk element made it impossible to sell the business.

Even if the lease is under the Landlord and Tenant Act, if it only has a few years left you may need to try and renew it before selling. This is because your buyer, particularly if they are a first timer, may need a lease that ties in with the length of their bank loan, which will usually be 10 or 15 years. The banks tend to be quite strict about this because they want to limit their lending risk.

On a few occasions I have come across pharmacies occupying premises on a licence and unfortunately this situation can poses problems. In one such case in Norfolk my client had occupied the premises for 29 years and was ready to retire. When I asked him about the lease he explained that it was on a licence with no proper lease in place.

I immediately saw a problem looming and put him in touch with an experienced property solicitor. Because it was a grey area in legal terms the solicitor took opinion from expert legal counsel who thought the situation might be legitimate, but could not be definitive.

On that basis we tried to sell the pharmacy and had interest from buyers but as soon as they approached their lenders the sale was aborted. During this time my client was negotiating with the landlord to get a proper lease put in place. Eventually the lease came through and the pharmacy was sold.

In this example my client first contacted me in October 2010 and the pharmacy sale was completed in July 2012. This illustrates the delays that can occur when there is an issue involving a third party landlord,

*whether it happens to be a licence that needs to be converted into a
suitable lease or simply a lease renewal.*

Allow plenty of time for lease renewals. There is no urgency for your
landlord to deal with your lease renewal, and typically it can take
months to process. If you recognise that your lease needs to be
renewed in order to sell your pharmacy start negotiations with the
landlord as soon as possible. I have known it take well over a year for
lease issues to be sorted out, with a consequent delay in the sale.
Trying to sell your pharmacy at the same time as sorting out problems
with your lease can have a detrimental effect on the sale. If a sale
drags on buyers tend to lose interest and there is a risk it will collapse.

Some health centre pharmacy leases are reasonable but I have come
across a number of issues you need to be alert to:

- Such leases are not always under the Landlord and Tenant
  Act. If there is no right of renewal it will be difficult to sell
  the pharmacy. This can usually be resolved by paying the
  landlord a premium and agreeing to an increased rent.
  While this is not an ideal solution, if you are in this situation
  it at least enables the problem to be resolved, allowing you
  to move on with your life.
- The rent is often linked to various indices which can result
  in huge increases over relatively short periods of time.
- Service charges can sometimes be substantial.

*I was selling a business in a health centre that, on the face of it, was
very attractive with a good turnover – until the terms of the lease were
examined in closer detail! It turned out that the fixed rent reviews in
combination with high service charges were unsustainable for the
business going forward and there was little that the vendor could do
about it.*

The effect of this was to knock a sizeable chunk off the goodwill
value. With hindsight, the pharmacy owners should have sought
professional advice before signing such an onerous lease.

If you have a third party landlord the lease will need to be transferred to the new owner unless the lease is in the name of your limited company and you are selling the company. You will need landlord consent where the lease does need to be assigned to the buyer. Your solicitor will deal with obtaining the landlord's consent. Usually the landlord will want reassurance about the financial credibility of their new tenant and may require bank references from them.

Whether you own a pharmacy in a health centre or a high street, be careful what you agree to if you need to renew your lease. Don't think that because you are selling up it won't matter how much the rent is or what the terms of the lease are. You will struggle to sell the pharmacy if you agree to terms that are too onerous for your potential buyers. It is also worth mentioning that the higher the rent the less the goodwill value of the business. This is because rent affects the bottom line profitability which forms the basis of the business valuation.

Whoever ends up buying your pharmacy will be looking for security of tenure; therefore leases need to be transferable and renewable with terms which are not prohibitive to the business. This has a huge impact on the saleability of a pharmacy and its goodwill value.

Key points for a successful sale

1. If you own the freehold of the pharmacy get an up-to-date valuation for the property carried out by a local commercial valuer.

2. If you have a lease with a third party landlord check the expiry date and terms. If it needs to be renegotiated start the process early before you put the pharmacy on the market.

CHAPTER 9

Marketing and confidentiality

A key factor to successfully selling your business is effective marketing: knowing the market and what buyers are looking for is imperative when you come to sell. Equally important is identifying who the serious buyers are, with the funding to buy your pharmacy. Knowing how to obtain the best price while cutting out time wasters and reducing the risk of confidentiality breaches is another vital ingredient to a successful sale.

Marketing your business

For most pharmacy owners it will be the first and last time that they sell a business, so there is only one chance to get it right. This underlines the importance of having an expert pharmacy agent to handle the sale for you. Some pharmacists think they can just announce that their pharmacy is for sale and the offers will come flooding in. It may be a seller's market but this approach is likely to attract poor offers from unqualified buyers, many of whom will not have sufficient finance to buy the business. Without proper preparation and presentation of the business buyers will make low offers.

Presentation

When you are ready to sell your agent, who should have carried out a detailed market appraisal of the business, will prepare the following:

- *Sales memorandum* This will include the main points about the business that are of importance to potential buyers.

The document should have enough information to whet their appetite. At this stage buyers don't want pages of waffle – they are looking for a brief summary of the business highlighting the key figures from your accounts such as turnover and gross profit.

- *Financial information pack* This will comprise of your accounts and other important financial documents such as your NHS statements.

These are the key documents in the marketing and sales process and will form the basis of the buyer's interpretation of the pharmacy business. They must be accurate and contain all the information a prospective buyer needs to know. Where a pharmacy is growing, or has only been trading for a short time, it may be appropriate to include projections of future turnover and profitability in order to demonstrate the value of the business.

This is also the time that any issues relating to the pharmacy or your financial documents should be disclosed to avoid misunderstandings or loss of trust later in the sale process. Good documentation and clear explanations will help the sales process to move forward quickly. If there is a potential problem regarding the business, such as a pending GP surgery move or an unusually high rent, it is probably not insurmountable, but now is the time to put it on the table. A good agent should have the experience to be able to advise you on your options and to help you find solutions. The crucial thing is to know your buyers, and your agent should make it their business to know who the right buyers are for your pharmacy.

A pharmacy I dealt with recently, which potentially could have been a difficult sale, was located in London. The rent paid for the premises was considerable, somewhere in the region of £45,000 a year. While a rent of this level is by no means unusual for London the problem was that the pharmacy made relatively little profit, and would struggle to pay a pharmacist's salary and cover a loan repayment. Banks are not keen to lend to businesses which can't generate enough profit to repay their loans! The premises were also in need of refurbishment.

Knowing the right buyers for this particular business helped, and I was able to generate significant interest in the pharmacy, obtaining five decent offers. The sale was completed promptly.

Selection of buyers

A good agent will have the contact details and be in touch with dozens of buyers who could be potential purchasers for your pharmacy. A key job for your agent is to carefully select and make a shortlist of the best candidates so that you are not troubled with time wasters. This also means that if you are concerned about confidentiality you will not have details of your business circulated to hundreds of people. The more people who are aware of the sale, the more likely it is that your staff will find out.

You may have particular people you want to include on the list: buyers who have contacted you in the past, or locums who work for you can all be included. You may also have people who you do not want to sell to and wish to exclude from the list.

Advertising

If you would like your pharmacy to be advertised your agent should be prepared to do this for you at no extra cost. However, they should only advertise the business is for sale with your permission. The place to advertise is in magazines such the *Pharmaceutical Journal* and *Chemist+Druggist*. An advertisement should only contain brief information such as turnover and the general location of a business in order to maintain confidentiality. Ultimately adverts are a great way to generate additional interest in the business and help to boost the price that can be achieved for you.

Keep an open mind...

Limiting your marketing can be seriously detrimental to achieving the best price for your business. Some sellers set criteria about who they do or do not wish to sell to. They may not want to sell to a multiple or the competition up the road, for example, when it is often these parties that will be willing to pay the highest price. It is advisable to keep an open mind and look at all options. Trust your agent to select the best buyers since this is what generates competition and what will achieve the best price. In the end, the choice of which offer to accept, even if it is not the highest, remains with you.

I had been marketing a group of pharmacies for a client, and despite my advice had been prohibited from sending the details to one particular individual who I had identified as being the most likely and best buyer.

In the event, a good offer was received and accepted from another buyer. Unfortunately, a few months down the line, the two parties could not agree on certain points and a stalemate situation arose with that purchaser.

Eventually an agreement was struck with the individual who had been denied information at the outset of the sale, but only after considerable time and legal fees had been spent with the previous purchaser.

Pharmacy viewings

Any buyer who is seriously interested in your business will want to meet with you and see the pharmacy. These viewings should be conducted at your convenience, which may be after hours in the evening or at weekends so as to maintain confidentiality and allow a quiet environment for discussion. From your perspective the purpose of the viewing is to meet the buyer and form an opinion as to whether you would like to sell to them.

The buyer will regard the meeting as an opportunity to obtain more information about the business. In some cases they may try and strike a deal with you there and then. You should not enter into any negotiations or accept any offers – just refer them back to your agent. Many buyers are quite astute. They know that if they can approach you directly with an offer and put a bit of pressure on you there's a chance they may be able to buy the pharmacy at a lower price than they would have to pay if they went through your agent.

Your only real contact with the buyer during the marketing process is likely to be at the viewing. One word of advice would be to think before you speak. Something you may regard as a selling point may actually be detrimental. You may be selling a business that has been in your family for generations, with a loyal customer base. You know all the local people well and they've been coming to your pharmacy for years. It may be natural to you to make a point of this when you are showing buyers around, however from a buyer's perspective it can be a negative factor. Their concern will be whether these customers will continue their patronage once the pharmacy has changed hands. Maybe they will give that new 100-hour pharmacy that opened a couple of years ago down the road a try!

Confidentiality

A major concern for many pharmacy owners is how to keep the sale confidential. Understandably, you may be worried that word will get out and staff may find out about the sale before you are ready to tell them. This is always a risk whether you are selling the business privately or through an agent, but it can be minimised and managed if properly handled. The use of confidentiality agreements helps with this and reinforces to potential buyers that they must keep details of the sale confidential.

If you are using an agent they should make sure that the buyers they are dealing with sign confidentiality agreements. The following is a sample agreement.

CONFIDENTIALITY AGREEMENT

This agreement is between XYZ Pharmacy Agency (being retained by the vendor as party to this agreement) and [prospective buyer]

Whose address is: (please complete)

[address]

The above parties agree as follows:-

1) To further the business relationship between XYZ Agency and the Recipient it is necessary that XYZ Agency discloses to the Recipient confidential information relating to business for whom XYZ Agency is acting as agents. The information relating to a vendor's business may include without limitation, trading accounts, trade secrets, future or proposed products or services, business forecasts, trading information and sales prospects, details of property investments etc.

XYZ Agency's sales information may be communicated orally, visually, in document form, by demonstration, or otherwise to the Recipient.

2) The Recipient shall prevent any unauthorised disclosure or publication of the XYZ Agency's information, and to keep the disclosed information confidential, and the Receiver shall not disclose the XYZ Agency's information to any third party, or reproduce the disclosure information in whole or in part without the prior approval from XYZ Agency. The recipient undertakes to make any employees, agents, advisory and family members of the Recipient aware of and comply to like extent with the obligations on the part of the Recipient contained in this Agreement.

3) The Recipient shall neither use the XYZ Agency's Information nor circulate it within its own organisation except and only to the extent necessary for:

a) Negotiations, discussions and consultations with personnel or authorised representatives of XYZ Agency; or

b) Any other purpose XYZ Agency may hereafter authorise.

Please initial _____ *Date* _____

(Recipient)

4) All information and materials, including, without limitation, business accounts, computer discs, documents, manuals, specifications, and data files furnished to the Recipient shall be and remain the property of XYZ Agency and be returned promptly at its request with all copies made thereof.

Signed for and on behalf of:

Company ....

(The Recipient) ....

Please print name...

Contact Telephone Number ....

Email ....

I use an agreement similar to this. In some cases I use a more detailed six page non-disclosure agreement to further protect clients.

Confidentiality can be breached, accidentally or otherwise, so it is a good idea to have a contingency plan if this situation occurs. Your staff may overhear phone conversations, or be suspicious of unusual callers. Uncertainty breeds fear, and they will want to know what's going on. Hopefully this won't happen, but be prepared and plan how you might deal with it.

At some point you are going to have to let people know that you are selling up. When you do it is up to you. Some pharmacy owners 'go public' before they even put the business on the market. I have had clients who have made a big event of it, hosting retirement parties for their staff and customers. At the other extreme, some vendors leave it until the last minute. I recall one case where the vendor said nothing until the sale had completed. The staff were told as the keys were being handed over to the new owner. They were angry and upset, not because the business had been sold, but because they had not been told! The new owner had a difficult situation to deal with and the staff remained antagonistic for many months following the sale. It was actually damaging to the business.

Many sellers choose to tell the staff when they have reached the point of agreeing the sale with a buyer. This can work well because the buyer can then be introduced to the staff which should put their minds at rest.

Vendors sometimes worry too much about how their staff will take the news. I have never heard of anyone who has had their staff walk out when they have made the announcement. I remember a group owner telling me about an aborted private sale he had been through. He and his wife wanted to retire and the sale was at an advanced stage. The buyer had been in to meet the staff and then the sale collapsed just before it was due to complete. The staff had felt sorry for him and his wife, and had been very supportive, he told me.

If you are of retirement age it usually doesn't come as a great surprise when you announce your retirement! I remember one case where an elderly staff member said to my client: "Thank goodness! I have been waiting for you to retire so that I can too... I didn't want to leave you in the lurch so I have been hanging on waiting for you to sell up."

Key points for a successful sale

1. Be open and honest with your potential buyers. It is better to table any issues early on as buyers will do their own due diligence and if something untoward is uncovered it will damage trust between you and your buyer.

2. Take the advice of your agent: they will have dealt with hundreds of sales and know the market inside out, so let them lead the sale.

3. If you are concerned about confidentiality, make sure buyers sign a confidentiality agreement at the outset.

CHAPTER 10

How many offers should I expect?

Every pharmacy is different, so the number of offers you can expect when you put your business up for sale will depend on factors such as:

- How the business is marketed and presented.
- The area in which you are located in the UK and where exactly your pharmacy is positioned locally in relation to GP surgeries and competitors.
- How your turnover is made up. Is it the usual 90:10 ratio of NHS and counter business, or perhaps you have high counter trade or a large proportion of your NHS turnover comes from care homes.
- The future potential of the business, and whether the pharmacy is affected by local developments which could have a positive or negative impact on the business.

From experience, I can usually assess how popular a pharmacy will be when I carry out the valuation. By the time I have completed the valuation I have a good feeling for the price to market the pharmacy at and who it may appeal to. This chapter focuses on gaining interest from potential buyers, generating competitive offers and achieving the best bids.

The guide price
You should keep an open mind about the final price a pharmacy will sell for. If you can generate a number of offers the price can go much higher than the guide price. For that reason I always explain to my clients that we will pick a guide price and seek offers

in excess of that figure. To put it in perspective, imagine going to an auction to buy a house. The auctioneer will set a guide price but if you were to ask him before the auction what price a particular property will actually sell for, he won't be able to tell you. He may think it will reach £X on a good day, or only go for £Y if there's not much interest but he will not be able to give you a definitive answer. It is a similar situation when selling a pharmacy: nobody can tell you exactly what price you will achieve. Everyone can have an opinion, but it will be up to the buyers to name and pay the price.

Before calling in offers you must allow sufficient time for the prospective buyers to receive all relevant information, and have the chance to view the pharmacy and meet the vendor. However, the sale should not be allowed to drag on for so long that buyers start to lose interest. Ideally I look to call in offers within a few weeks of the business being marketed.

The number of offers

In the sellers' market that we are currently in, the number of offers received on a pharmacy sale is typically around four or five. Depending on the level of interest in your particular business, you could receive as many as 15 offers, as in a recent sale I handled. The shop in question did need a lick of paint, but on the whole it was a safe, profitable business and the response received was exceptional. The final sale price was well in excess of what had been anticipated. This shows the number of offers that a business which appeals to a wide range of purchasers can attract. In this case, first time buyers were interested as well as local pharmacy owners and small groups in the area which were looking to expand. The vendor allowed me to market the pharmacy fully, which meant I was able to generate significant interest. It also makes a big difference if the pharmacy is marketed at the right price level. If a pharmacy is overpriced interest in it is likely to be minimal, killing the sale.

A health centre pharmacy sale I handled recently in the Northampton area received offers ranging from £2m to £3m for the goodwill. When I originally carried out the valuation the net profit of the business (EBITDA) suggested a valuation based on profit of just over £2m. However, I knew that since this was a desirable health centre business in a good location we should be looking at a considerable premium on this for the final price.

With this in mind I put a guide price of offers over £2.5 million on the business, a premium of around £500,000 on the valuation. Due to the level of interest I opted for an initial round of offers followed by a final round. This is what happened:

- *Round 1*

Twelve offers received ranging from £2m to £2.8m.

- *Round 2*

Buyers were now aware of how strong the competition was for the business, and the offers we received ranged from £2.6m to £3m.

Where there is a lot of interest in a business I will often have two rounds of offers so that buyers can increase their original offer if they wish to do so. This ensures that the best offers have been made for the business.

To highlight the range of offers that can be made on the same business, here are some recent examples:

	Lowest offer	Highest offer	% difference
London	£1.475m	£2.072m	41%
Staffordshire	£1.2m	£1.950m	62%
Leicestershire	£1m	£1.3m	30%

It is always an advantage to have a few offers on the table. If the top offer doesn't materialise you are then in the fortunate position of having other parties that have appraised the business to fall back on. This situation is also useful in preventing the successful bidder from seeking to introduce any unreasonable terms into the contract of sale. If they are aware that other purchasers are in the wings and ready to move, they will know that you are less likely to tolerate unreasonable terms and conditions.

Unfortunately not all pharmacies generate multiple offers and a premium price. Some may only generate two or three offers. In these cases I would usually invite initial offers to come in by a specific date and then negotiate individually with each buyer to achieve their best and final offer. In rare cases only one offer might be made, in which case it may be necessary to proceed more cautiously to negotiate the best price from that buyer.

How do buyers view the offers process?

Buyers don't like being put in a situation where they are bidding against each other. This is bad news for them as they will have to pay a higher price than if they were negotiating on a one-to-one basis. Nevertheless they have to accept that with a shortage of pharmacies for sale they will have competition and if they want to buy they will have to take part in a bidding process.

A buyer wants to buy your pharmacy at the lowest possible price while negotiating the best terms and conditions for themselves. Who is in a stronger negotiating position – you or the buyer? If you have more than one offer you are in a good position; more than two offers you are in a strong position and with multiple offers you really are in a position of power! Buyers will seek to discover the minimum price that you are prepared to accept for the pharmacy, but you should never reveal your bottom line. A buyer is never going to go above this price point if it comes out, and they will use it as an opportunity to chip away at the price.

Buyers' negotiating tactics vary but generally they won't give their best price in their initial offer. I would expect to see an increase after some discussion or negotiation. The difficulty is knowing when the buyer has genuinely given you their final offer. There have been many occasions where a buyer has told me that they have made their final offer. When I decline this on behalf of the vendor, either because there is a better offer from someone else or it is unacceptably low, they suddenly find more money and come back with a new offer!

Don't be upset if you receive a low offer: you just need to move on. It may be that the buyer genuinely doesn't think your pharmacy is worth as much as you are asking for it, or they may be playing a game to see how low a price you will accept.

It is important to gain the buyer's trust as this makes the negotiations which lie ahead easier. I believe in being honest and upfront with buyers from the start of each sale. It's best to let the buyers know if there is an issue with the pharmacy before they put in their offers. I have dealt with vendors who, when they meet buyers, make up fictitious offers which they claim to have received. This kind of deception is likely to be uncovered by the buyers, with a consequent breakdown of trust and damage to the sale. I have also had vendors who tell buyers that they want a ridiculously high price for their business. The vendor thinks they are being clever in trying to push the buyer up, but it has the opposite effect and puts the buyer off. I then have an angry buyer to contend with who feels they have wasted their time viewing the pharmacy.

Most buyers will hold back their offer until the closing date, and often until the final hours of it. However, with two rounds for offers it would be unusual if no one increased their bid in the second round. This means that if several people have submitted offers in round one there is still the prospect of negotiating a higher price in round two.

Sometimes buyers try to apply pressure by putting a proviso on their offer. They may say that they need an answer within five days or their offer will be withdrawn. My job then is to weigh up the situation and try to gauge whether they are bluffing or if there is a genuine reason why the offer is time limited. The buyer could, for example, be in negotiation with another pharmacy and have to make a decision about where to commit.

The agent's angle

From my perspective I need to understand the buyers I deal with, from their financial position to their motivation for acquiring a particular pharmacy. The strength of their finances and motivation will affect the price they offer. You may have someone who is desperate to buy a particular pharmacy but they can't raise sufficient money, so the motivation is there but the finance is lacking. Conversely you can have a cash buyer who has the funds but their motivation may only be as strong as getting the business at a good price.

If a buyer has bought through me before or even made offers in the past I will know them and how they operate. This has made me wary of some buyers and question whether they will follow through on their offer if it is accepted. That said, there are many excellent buyers whom I have confidence in. For me part of the offers process is to build up a picture of each buyer and their credibility, and evaluate their offer in terms of price, terms and conditions of sale, and their financial position. This information helps the vendor make an informed decision on whose offer to accept.

What should the offer look like?

I insist that offers are submitted in a similar format to allow for easy comparison and to prevent any misunderstandings. You need to know exactly what the buyer is offering to buy. Are they making an offer for the shares in your company or just the assets in the business, and if so which assets? Sometimes a buyer can word the offer in an ambiguous way, and at this stage of the sale you have to be absolutely clear on exactly what is being bought and sold.

The offer for a pharmacy business should generally be for cash on completion of sale. Pharmacy sales differ from many other types of business sale where a sum is paid up front and the remainder over a period of years dependant on various factors. If a buyer offers you 50 per cent of the sale price on completion and the remainder over a couple of years I would find that unacceptable. I have known pharmacists who have done this because they have felt sorry for a first time buyer who was struggling to raise finance, but just remember that all the risk is with you. If the buyer runs the business into the ground and can't pay off their debts you will be the loser.

Occasionally there may be an agreement to stage payments over a period of years but this would only normally be put in place where there is a problem with the pharmacy that is likely to affect the future of the business. An example of this is where your local surgery is about to move, and the choice may be either to accept a ridiculously low offer or try and structure a payment schedule dependant on what happens to the business.

At the offer stage it is important to agree the big points such as the price, what's included, the basic structure of the sale, time scales and a target completion date. It is not advisable to get bogged down with the details at this point – they can be ironed out later.

Key points for a successful sale

1. Keep an open mind about the price.

2. The business must be properly marketed to quality buyers to generate good offers.

3. Make sure you fully understand the offers received for your pharmacy. It can be an expensive mistake to think you are selling your whole company only to discover just before completion that the offer was actually only for some of the assets in the company.

CHAPTER 11

What next after the sale is agreed?

Once the sale has been agreed it is essential, if you have not already done so, to instruct a solicitor who is familiar with pharmacy sales. Choosing a solicitor who is inexperienced in this area will extend the sale and will ultimately end up costing you more. I have seen this happen many times and it causes frustration and stress for both the seller and the buyer as the sale drifts past the deadlines agreed at the outset. Cheap advice is not necessarily the best advice. Pharmacy sale contracts need to include special clauses, so select a solicitor for their knowledge and experience of pharmacy sales, not their price. It will save you time and money in the long run.

I recall one case where the vendor's solicitor was so inexperienced that he downloaded a sales contract from the internet to use for his client's company share sale. Share purchase agreements are typically about 70 pages long but this solicitor had found a two page document written with American jargon which he was trying to use for his client's transaction!

Heads of terms

When you and the buyer have chosen your solicitors the next stage is to draw up the heads of terms (subject to contract). This document should spell out clearly and concisely the key terms and structure of the deal so that there is no confusion later on. Although this is not a binding agreement it represents the intentions of both buyer and seller.

When I am acting for the vendor I will prepare this document on their behalf, but it could be prepared by your solicitor or even the buyer's solicitor. I find that doing it myself means the sale gets underway quickly, whereas when solicitors are asked to construct the document they tend to start negotiating on points which would normally be dealt with later in the main sale and purchase agreement. You want the heads of terms prepared and agreed promptly because this document should include a time scale for the sale and provision for the buyer to pay an up-front deposit (if that was agreed when the buyer made their offer).

You may wish to grant the buyer a period of exclusivity in return for their deposit. The period of exclusivity would normally be for three or four months, giving them time to do their due diligence, to have the sale purchase agreement prepared and agreed, and to ensure their finance is available. Obtaining a deposit should indicate to you that the buyer is serious. The exclusivity period shows goodwill to the purchaser because the pharmacy is off the market completely during this period.

Once the heads of term are prepared they should be circulated to all relevant parties – the buyer, the seller, both sets of solicitors, and any other advisers such as accountants.

Legal contracts

From the outset always give your solicitor clear instructions. They need to understand your objectives and time scales. Your solicitor should provide you with a list of the information that they need from you (see Chapter 7). This information is necessary for the legal due diligence, which is the process of answering the buyer's enquiries relating to the business and the property. It is best practice for the seller to be as thorough and helpful as possible when responding to these enquiries, and to assist in the disclosure exercise (see below).

You should also expect the buyer's accountant to carry out financial due diligence on the business, and the buyer to carry out commercial due diligence. Try and forward all the requested information to your solicitor on a timely basis. Make it clear and comprehensive so that it is easy for your solicitor to understand and present to the buyer's solicitor. This should reduce the number of further queries from the buyer's side and may even help to minimise your legal fees!

Property and leases

If you have a landlord, your solicitor should approach them as early as possible after agreeing the sale for consent to assign the lease. This is an important point because it can take some time, being dependent on your landlord's own representatives. An Energy Performance Certificate, and fire safety and asbestos certificates may also be required. If the inspections needed for these certificates have not been carried out already you may have to organise them at your expense.

If you own the freehold and your intention is to set up a new lease for your buyer, your solicitor can draft this at the outset of the legal process. An experienced pharmacy solicitor will have a good idea of standard pharmacy leases and is likely to have a suitable template. You should check that your solicitor is actually working on this and that it doesn't get left until the last minute. I have been in a situation where I thought the sale was ready to complete when suddenly it transpired that the solicitor's property department hadn't even started work on the lease!

> *I had a situation recently where my client owned the premises and I was expecting his solicitor to prepare a new lease for the pharmacy's buyer. On chasing up the solicitor for the new lease I was met with the response that they were waiting for me to do it. When I pointed out to them that this was their job, they said they didn't know who could do it, and they would have to outsource it! This disappointing situation again emphasises the importance of having legal representatives who can do the job.*

Buyer's bank valuations

If you own the freehold of the business and are including this in the sale, then be prepared for the buyer to require their own independent valuation of the property. I always make sure that the buyer gets this underway early in the sale process so that if any issues arise they can be addressed promptly.

In addition to a valuation of the property, in almost every sale the buyer's lender will want to carry out a valuation of the pharmacy goodwill. This is done by the bank as security to ensure the business can support the loan amount, and will be carried out by a specialist valuer. You will need to put aside some time to answer the valuer's questions about the business. You can meet the valuer at the pharmacy if you are happy to do so and the staff are aware of the sale, or at a more private location nearby, in which case the valuer may have carried out a discreet 'mystery shop' of the pharmacy in advance.

This valuation should also be carried out promptly at the outset of the sale to ensure that there will not be any issues with the funding. The valuer will need to be provided with details of the business and the financial information pack prior to carrying out the valuation. Be mindful when you are speaking to the valuer and answering any questions that they are looking for a business that supports loan repayments for the new buyer after you have sold.

Sale and purchase agreement

The sale and purchase agreement is legally binding once it is signed. It should set out all the terms of the sale, so it is important to ensure it adequately protects your position. It is usual practice for the buyer's solicitor to prepare the first draft of this agreement, although I have had occasions where the vendor's solicitor has done so. Tactically there can be reasons to ask your solicitor to draft the agreement. If you suspect the buyer's solicitor is inexperienced in this type of legal work it may be beneficial for your solicitor to take control of the contract and dictate the terms.

The agreement is likely to contain obligations on you as the seller, such as not to compete with the business after completion for a period of time, usually two to three years.

The buyer will require warranties and indemnities from you covering all aspects of the business. Warranties are guarantees from you regarding the pharmacy and its assets at completion which the buyer can rely on. If any of the warranties prove to be untrue the buyer will have a right to claim against you, unless the matter was notified to the buyer in sufficient detail before completion during the disclosure exercise (see below).

There should also be provisions limiting your liability if a claim is brought by the buyer because, for example, a warranty proves to be untrue. These limitations set restrictions on the circumstances where the buyer can bring a warranty claim (for example, the buyer may be prevented from bringing a warranty claim after a certain period of time). Indemnities establish the liability that can arise if problems are discovered after the sale completes.

If you are selling the shares in your limited company, the buyer will require a tax deed. This obliges you as the seller to reimburse the buyer for any tax outside of the ordinary that the company has to pay after completion, but it only applies to the company's business up until completion.

Disclosure exercise

This disclosure usually consists of a letter addressed to the buyer. Its purpose is to serve as a source of specific information for the buyer in addition to that already provided during the due diligence process. It also serves to minimise the risk to you of a claim being brought against you for a breach of the warranties.

Your solicitor should try and manage your exposure to indemnity and warranty claims as far as possible by building some protection into your sales agreement in terms of the amount which can be claimed, together with a time scale for making a claim.

Retention

With a company share sale the buyer will often request a retention on completion of the sale. This is where money is held back from the completion proceeds pending certain outcomes. There may be a retention until the final completion accounts are agreed, for example, which will typically be three or four months after the sale completes. The amount retained will depend on the negotiating skills of your advisers. There may also be a retention for a year or two of part of the sale proceeds in case any claims arise against the business you have sold. Again, the amount of the retention will depend on negotiation but it should not be more than 10 per cent of the sale price and usually should not be retained for more than one year after the sale.

The agent's role

If you are using a pharmacy agent they should be very active during this stage of the sale, liaising with you, the buyer and all the respective advisers to ensure the sale completes as quickly as possible. Frequently there are points that require negotiation during the legal process and your agent is in the best position to assist with this because they have the best over view of the situation. They can liaise with all parties involved and ensure matters are resolved quickly. A good agent should also assist where necessary with NHS change of ownership and fitness to practice applications.

Procrastination is not your friend

Do not think that, because you have agreed a price, completing the legal paperwork is just a formality. There is no guarantee at this stage that the sale will go through. In fact, the longer a sale drags on the more likely it is to fail. Below are a few examples I have seen of why sales have fallen through:

- A lengthy delay caused by an inexperienced solicitor gave the buyer time to reconsider their options and decide not to proceed.
- A Category M clawback announcement severely affected the pharmacy's value, resulting in the sale being aborted.
- The uncertainty arising from the news that the local doctors were relocating caused the buyer to withdraw from the sale.
- The buyer's finance was withdrawn by the bank after the sale was delayed because a third party landlord took too long to negotiate a new lease.

- The sale was delayed because the buyer's 'fitness to practice' approval took months to obtain. During this time the seller had lost interest in the business leading to a drop in turnover. When the buyer was able to complete he conducted a final review of the business, discovered the decreased turnover and pulled out of the sale.
- Delays by the seller in providing information frustrated the buyer so much that they found an alternative pharmacy to buy.

And remember, if you have not told your staff about the sale, the longer the transaction takes the more likely it is that news of it will leak out!

Miscellaneous points for consideration

There are other points you may need to consider as a part of the sale process:

- If you or any of your business partners or existing directors continue to work in the business following completion the buyer may require you to sign up to new terms of employment.
- It will be necessary under TUPE regulations to consult with the employees of the business before completion if the sale is not a sale of a limited company.
- A stock take is likely to be needed and it should take place at, or soon after, completion. This will need to be booked in advance as stock takers become busy towards the end of the month, and particularly busy at the end of the tax year. Usually an independent stock taker will be jointly instructed and the cost split between you and the buyer.
- While on the subject of stock, the buyer may ask for a cap to be put on the stock to be transferred on completion of the sale. This can be the subject of negotiation but it is better to reach agreement as soon as possible so that you have time to run down stock levels if required before the sale completes.

- The General Pharmaceutical Council and NHS local area team must be notified of the sale and approve any transfer of ownership and 'fitness to practice' applications. Transfer of ownership will depend on whether the contract and premises are registered to a company or a sole trader.
- If the NHS contract is in the company name and you are selling the company you should not need to transfer ownership. Where applicable, the transfer of ownership for the pharmacy contract should be applied for as soon as is practical after the sale has been agreed as it can take up to 90 days to fully approve. There may also be 'fitness to practice' checks required for the buyer.
- If you are selling a company check that the NHS contract is in the company name. I have come across a number of cases where the pharmacy owner started off as a sole trader with the contract in their own name, and later converted to a limited company but forgot to transfer the contract into the company. If this applies to you it is not a problem but it does mean that the contract will need to be transferred to the company prior to completion of the sale. This needs to be dealt with early on in the sale process to avoid delays.
- Do not assume 'fitness to practice' approval will be a formality for the buyer. Obviously it depends on who the buyer is but I have seen delays and issues with buyers getting this approval.
- Many properties are situated in flood risk areas. If this applies to your pharmacy it may be an issue for the buyer. You could commission an independent flood risk report and you may be able to obtain commercial property flood insurance.
- You probably have service contracts with various suppliers. Make sure you check these prior to completion and take any necessary actions. For example, what is going to happen to equipment such as your dispensary PMR system and EPOS? Does the buyer wish to take this on, and if so will the supplier allow the contract to be transferred?
- If the buyer is acquiring your company the contracts will

remain in the company name so there shouldn't be anything to transfer. However, the buyer may have their own systems and not require yours, in which case it will be up to you to terminate the agreements and settle any costs involved.

Finally, ensure you keep the pharmacy running normally and the turnover levels constant. The offer to buy is made on the information given at the outset of the sale, so it is expected that on completion this will not have changed for the worse. Remember the deal is not done until you receive the money, so don't take your eye off the ball!

Key points for a successful sale

1. Be prompt in providing all the information required by your solicitor.

2. Don't assume that the sale is progressing quickly. Keep chasing your solicitor for updates and make sure the buyer is dealing with everything on a timely basis.

3. If you have an agent acting for you make sure they are overseeing the sale properly.

CHAPTER 12

Time scales for selling

The $64,000 dollar question that I am regularly asked at the outset of a sale is: 'How long will it take?' With so many factors that can affect a sale the best I can do is to take you though each stage and look at the likely scenarios. For this purpose I have split the sale into two parts: the first is the period up to the point the sale is agreed, and the second covers the legal process through to completion.

Part 1 – To when the sale is agreed

Weeks 1-4
You have decided that you are ready to sell your pharmacy, so you phone a pharmacy agent to discuss this and request a valuation. The agent will request information that you will need to prepare and forward – this may take you a week or so. The agent will then review the information and prepare the valuation which is discussed with you. Expect this to take another week or so. We are already 3– 4 weeks down the road.

Weeks 5–6
You instruct the agent. They visit you and prepare a sales memorandum and document pack, and select suitable buyers to market the business to.

Weeks 7–12
The marketing process gets underway when buyers receive details of your pharmacy, come and see you, and offers are called in.

There may be a period of negotiation with the buyer before a price is agreed, along with the terms and conditions of sale.

So far it has taken around 12 weeks to reach the stage where a sale is agreed. Can you reduce the time this takes? Time can be saved in the initial valuation stage of weeks 1-4. If you have all your financial information to hand and can email this straight over to your agent the same or next day, and ask the agent to prioritise the valuation for you, it is possible to reduce this stage to a few days and so save up to three weeks in this part of the process.

Six weeks has been allowed for the marketing process, but it is possible to agree a sale in less time. I have agreed a sale in a day where the pharmacy owner was in severe financial difficulties, but this is not ideal if you wish to obtain the best price! You need to give buyers sufficient time to make a considered decision. Bear in mind that key buyers may be on holiday or their advisers may not be immediately available. You can push ahead without offers from key buyers, but you risk leaving money on the table. If everything goes smoothly and the buyers are able to make their offers on a timely basis you could cut this stage down to 3-4 weeks.

Overall, the first part of the sale can be reduced from around 12 weeks to about six weeks if your essential information is already collated and everything else falls into place. However, it is more realistic to set your expectations to a 12 week time scale.

Part 2 – Through to completion

Weeks 13-24
Once the sale has been agreed the next step is to prepare the heads of terms outlining the main points agreed with the buyer such as price, and specific terms and conditions. I usually allow about a week for this and for the deposit (if applicable) to be paid by the buyer.

After this comes the start of the legal process, and this is where lots of delays and unexpected issues can arise. If everything goes to plan this stage should take no more than 12 weeks, but since many more people are now involved there is more scope for delay. The buyer, the seller, both sets of solicitors, accountants, valuers, banks and possibly the local NHS team could all be engaged. This is a large group, and ensuring they are communicating effectively with each other and co-ordinating their activity can be a daunting task. During a three month period people may go on holiday, be off sick, and have a heavy workload – all things that can contribute to delaying the completion of your sale.

In addition to this other issues can arise which will delay the sale, such as:

- *Solicitors* An inexperienced or slow solicitor will at best delay the sale and at worst wreck it. I still come across solicitors who insist on sending everything by post: this alone can prolong the sale by weeks. I sometimes have clients who are reluctant to chase their solicitor for fear of pushing up their costs, and have on one occasion been instructed not to contact a solicitor for this reason. This is a ridiculous situation! When you are selling possibly the biggest asset you own your priority should be to progress the sale as quickly as possible to completion, not trying to save a few hundred pounds in legal fees.

- *NHS England/Wales/Scotland* Bear in mind that if you are selling via an asset sale a change of ownership is required which can take a month or sometimes longer to be approved by the NHS. The time taken to handle applications varies, however the 30 days appeal process is standard. If you need to apply for change of ownership this needs to be put in progress soon after the sale has been agreed to avoid delays.

- *Leasehold property* In the case of leasehold properties the landlord needs to re-assign the lease to the purchaser and this can be a slow process. To speed things up the landlord and their agent should be warned in advance of the impending transfer. The landlord will require information regarding their new tenant (your buyer) such as accounts and references. The exact requirements should be conveyed to the buyer and applied for as early as possible, since in some cases banks can be particularly slow at providing references.

Landlords and their agents can make unreasonable requests and be slow to act on information provided to them. In light of this, the sooner the transfer proceedings are started, the better. It is better to be ready for completion early than to try and rush the deal.

- *Lender's requirements* The buyer's bank may decide that it wants to see interim management accounts or the latest set of accounts, which may not be ready if your year end has only just passed. This can delay the sale for a few weeks.

A good agent can cut the time down for the sale process because they will be making sure everyone is working to a timetable. They will ensure that all parties are liaising with each other, that documents and information are submitted on time, that NHS applications are correctly completed and property surveys and valuations carried out quickly. Properly done, this will cut the time taken at each stage and minimise the stress levels for all those involved in the sale.

From the time table above you will see that, on average, a sale will take about six months from start to finish providing no important issues arise to cause a delay. The sale can be completed in a shorter time frame but everything needs to click into place for that to happen.

Private sales

The process described above assumes you are using an agent to handle the sale. You may be wondering what the time scale might be if you are selling your business privately. From discussions I have had with pharmacy owners who have either attempted or managed to sell privately it seems the sale itself is agreed relatively quickly. If you are only talking to one buyer this part of the process should not be time consuming.

However things frequently go wrong or there are substantial delays once the sale progresses to the legal stage. It is not unusual to hear of delays ranging from months to a year or more, with the sale often eventually collapsing (see Chapter 6 for more on private sales).

In conclusion

Unfortunately, pharmacy sales rarely go exactly to plan. The best advice I can give you is to appoint a first class team of advisers whom you can depend on and who will guide you through the process and look after your best interests.

Key points for a successful sale

1. Agreeing a time table with your buyer and solicitors is crucial to keeping the sale on track.

2. Keep on top of the sale by being in regular contact with your buyer, solicitor and any other advisers involved in the sale.

3. Be prepared for issues to arise during the sale which will require negotiation and discussion.